Murder and Mayhem in Dallas County

Murder and Mayhem in Dallas County
Copyright © 2019 by Mike Flinn
Panther Creek Publishing
Box 188
Adel, Iowa 50003

All rights reserved. No part of this book may be reproduced or used in any manner without the express written permission of the publisher except for the use of brief quotations in a book review Specific quotes, pictures, descriptions, articles and other work that is copyrighted by other parties is not included in this copyright

ISBN: 9781707672820

Imprint: Independently published

Panther Creek Publishing Co.
P.O. Box 188
Adel, Iowa 50003
ironpdlr@gmail.com

Books may be purchased in quantity and/or special sales by contacting the publisher, Mike Flinn, at PO Box 188, Adel, Iowa 50003 or by e-mail at <u>ironpdlr@gmail.com</u>.

© by the author of this book. The book author retains sole copyright to his or her contributions to this book.

Other Books by Mike Flinn

Most Exciting Day

A Soldier's Bounty

The Silent Cannons

The Threshing Crew

Hard Times and the Raccoon's Tale

An Old Codger's Take

Whisky Money

2019 ironpdlr@gmail.com

First Edition   Printed in U.S.A.

This Book is Dedicated to the people of Dallas County Who, From the Beginning, Have Cherished and Maintained Law and Order and Endeavored to Keep Dallas County a Safe Place to Live

Foreward

I could use up space and bore you mercilessly by discussing crime rates, types of crime (violent as opposed to property), and where Dallas County stands in relation to similar sized counties. But that's not what this book is about. This book is about the history of Dallas County and some of the incidents in its more colorful past. I hope that you will find stories here that are tragic, sad, amusing, disgusting, interesting, informative and maybe even all of the above.

Like every other inhabited territory of its size, Dallas County had its share of rascals, scoundrels and downright heartless and evil people through the years. But we have also been blessed, from the beginning, with outstanding law enforcement personnel that have the support of the county and its citizens. There is no better proof of that support than the new law Enforcement Center, that is currently under construction east of the county seat of Adel.

But just so you won't be left wondering, here are the crime statistics for Dallas County. On a scale of 1 to 100, Dallas County violent crime is 13.0 (The US average is 22.7). Property crime is 20.6 (The US average is 35.4). These figures should help us all sleep better at night.

Contents

Chapter	Title	Page
One	*In the Beginning*	1
Two	*John Bold*	15
Three	*The Unfortunate Case of Jasper Mason*	19
Four	*Adel's Most Exciting Day*	27
Five	*The Van Meter Visitor*	73
Six	*Call Out the Dogs*	79
Seven	*Unsolved John Doe Murder of 1905*	85
Eight	*Prohibition and the Roaring Twenty's*	89
Nine	*Boonville Bandits*	107
Ten	*Murder of Fred Wernli*	113
Eleven	*Virgil Untied and the Minburn Shootout*	121

Twelve...........*Attacked with an Axe*...................…........127

Thirteen…........*Bonnie and Clyde at Dexter*.….....…....131

Fourteen….... *The Dirty Thirty's*............….......…....149

Fifteen….........*Mystery Skull*.................…....….....161

Sixteen….…......*The Forty's and Fifty's*..............…....169

Seventeen….....*Minburn Bank Robbery*................…...183

Eighteen….......*Murder Among the Tropical Fish*..…......195

Nineteen…........*The Try-Angle Inn Murder*.............…..199

Twenty….....…*The Shy Quiet Victim...Emma Lewis*........207

Twenty-One...*The Murder House*........................….....211

Twenty-Two....*Gregg Nimmo*.............….......….........231

Twenty-Three..*Sheriffs of Dallas County*..................235

The Old Jail... North of Courthouse

Drawing of New Law Enforcement Facility

Chapter One

In the Beginning

To begin this journey through Dallas County's more unruly history, let us go back approximately 200 years to a time before Dallas County was Dallas County. We would be in the Iowa Territory on land that would soon become Dallas County. It's a scenic land, unspoiled by roads, fields, railroads, real estate and political signs, houses, towns or even people. The open lands are covered with grasses and prairie flowers. Along the streams are all the trees that are native to this land, ash, hickory, elm, oak, maple, walnut and cottonwood.

There is abundant animal life too. Flocks of geese, ducks, prairie chickens, turkeys and quail can be seen. Herds of bison graze the prairie while the woods are teeming with deer, raccoons, wolves, badgers and even panthers.

The only human inhabitants of this land are Native Americans. Although many tribes made their temporary homes here, only two were known to permanently inhabit this peaceful land, the Sauk and Fox. These people built their wigwams by setting a circle of small poles and covering them with skins and bark. In winter, they built their fires in the middle of these wigwams and cooked their food in earthen pots suspended over the flames. These dwellings, in the middle of January,

Chapter One: In the Beginning

must have been smokier than a working man's tavern on payday before the smoking ban.

Much like today, the men enjoyed hunting, fishing and trapping. They also enjoyed the fact that their women did much of the real work, cooking, child-care and planting the ground to raise a good portion of their food supply. Even though the Indian was an alert and able hunter, much of their diet was provided by the wife and squaw's more agrarian pursuits. These early farmers tilled the rich Dallas County soil and raised corn, beans and vegetables.

It wasn't all as serene and peaceful as one might imagine, however. The Indian was accustomed to wondering the land, taking game wherever he pleased. He was rugged, fearless and cruel, and had a great passion for war.

It's 1841, and a large band of approximately 1600 Sauk and Fox Indians are at their camp along the east side of the Des Moines River near the mouth of the Raccoon. Today this location would be near downtown Des Moines. It's late August or early September and, as the sun is setting in the west, the rhythmic beating of drums can be heard for miles along the riverbanks. A great war dance is taking place.

Suddenly an excited and exhausted Delaware warrior comes bounding into the campfire sight. He is shouting the news of a terrible event, the murder of about two dozen other Delaware warriors by members of the Sioux tribe. The Delaware Chief, Neswage, was among those killed. This lone Delaware warrior was the only survivor. The slaughtered Delawares were on their way here to this camp to visit their friends, the Sauk and Fox, when the massacre occurred.

Keokuk, Pashepaho and Kishchosk, chiefs of the Sauk and Fox, were with the tribes. Pashepaho, although pushing 80 years old and too weak to mount his horse unassisted, put on his war paint and proceeded to lead a band of about 600 mounted warriors. Also, along with them were three palefaces, John Evans, Thomas Connelly and James Ewing, all from the trading post at Fort Des Moines.

The Delaware warrior led them up the Raccoon River to the place where the Sioux had attacked the Delawares. The scene of this Indian massacre was just north of where the City of Adel now sits in what would soon become Dallas County. It was a grizzly scene. They found the body of Neswage, the Delaware chief, lying by a tree with his tomahawk by his side. There were four Sioux warrior bodies by the tree that had been slain by Chief Neswage. The trunk of the tree had many scars from repeated blows. The party also found the bodies of 22 other Delawares and 26 Sioux that had been slain during the fighting.

Angered by this bloody deed, the Indians decided to pursue the miscreants. They continued on without Evans, Connelly and Ewing and overtook the Sioux about 100 miles north of where the massacre had occurred. Another bloody battle was fought, resulting in the death of 300 Sioux warriors. The victorious Sauk and Fox lost only seven of their own braves. There's no doubt they had revenged the death of their friends, the Delawares.

The area is now known simply as "The Island," but it might well be called "Battle Island." The people of Adel might be missing an opportunity to create a new tourist trap.

This was, perhaps, the last Indian battle in Iowa. Leonard Brown was a Des Moines schoolteacher who, when he wasn't teaching the ABC's, liked to write poetry. He probably obtained the story of the Battle of Adel from Alexander R. Fulton, author of "The Red Men of Iowa." Brown memorialized in verse this little-remembered Indian massacre in Dallas County.

PASH-E-PA-HO

By: LEONARD BROWN

Inscribed to My Friend, John Evans March 20, 1878

The Delaware chief, Nes-wa-ge, encamped over night near the timber
North of the beautiful site of Adel, all then a wild prairie.
Gracefully waved the tall grass on the lowlands adjoining the river;
Mower nor scythe had disturbed it. The deer and the elk and the bison

Chapter One: In the Beginning

Grazed on those grass-covered plateaus; while the huts of the beaver (Washed by the Raccoon—Asipala, the swift-flowing water) Marked here the only fixed habitations since the mound builders' era.

Promptly at dawn rise Nes-wa-ge and band. The twenty-four warriors

Catch up their ponies, that all night had regaled on the bluestem.

Now the braves breakfast; jerked buffalo-beef and broiled venison, the viands.

Shall they start on their journey again. to the "big-smoke-for-horses"?

Shall ever greet them the Sauks and Mas-qua-kies that wait their arrival? •

Six hundred warriors (the tribe sixteen hundred with women and children)

Happy this morning arose with the sun that looked red in his anger.

Loudly the bugle at dawning proclaimed to the soldiers' reveille;

Wakened the slumbering dragoons to roll-call and coffee.

Floats o'er the log barrack at Fort Des Moines the star-spangled emblem;

Two lovely rivers uniting in marriage rejoice to behold it. High on the hill-tops the walnut and hickory, majestic as sachems.

Give to the red men rich fruit and sad music in autumn.

Children of Nature, ye bask in the sunshine of balmy September,

Watching the wild geese fly southward and fishes dart through the water.

"Lazy your lives," say the cynics, "and aimless and useless as lazy."

Sorrow moans in the treetops above you, requiems of sadness.

Dark is the threatening future; but little regard ye the morrow.

Care ever greets you as kindly as guardian angels do children;

Mild as the morning of summer, she smites you how gently with kisses!

Gather for council Kis-ka-kosh, Ke-o-kuk and the brave Nash-e-wes-kuk

(Black Hawk's son, "Thé Daring"), and Pash-e-pa-ho, "The Stabber,"

Friend of the Delawares (he truly loved as a brother Neswa-ge).

Other great chiefs of the Sauks and Mus-qua-kies are present;

Ne-Pope (Black-Hawk's lieutenant), Oppe-Noose, and the war chief Wa-pel-law,

Others less noted—their names are too numerous for mention.

Thus Pash-e-pa-ho: "A banquet of welcome we give to the Delawares;

Soon will be with us Nes-wa-ge and braves from o'er the Big Muddy;

Presents befitting are ready—an outfit of excellent ponies

Give them the best. Let this be a great feast—a 'big-smoke-for-horses.' "

Pash-e-pa-ho's grim face wears the scars of innumerable deep wounds.

Proud is the chieftain of these as a schoolgirl is proud of her tresses.

Hideous his countenance—still he's beloved by all the young warriors.

Four score winters have frosted the scalp-lock of brave Pash-e-pa-ho;

Twenty-four pale-faces have paled 'neath the blows of his hatchet;

Seventy-two fierce Da-ko-tas have yielded their lives to his valor;

Ninety-six ugly scalps he wears 'round his neck as a garland.

So, when in war dance Pash-e-pa-ho "The Stabber," steps forward.

Boasting his prowess—his conquests—the foes he has slaughtered.

Braves crowd the circle and cover his mouth with a wolfskin—

Chapter One: In the Beginning

Mark of high honor, as if to say, "Bravé man, keep silent; You, Pash-e-pa-ho, make our deeds seem by contrast as nothing."

Smokes, in the soup-bowls of bass-wood, the banquet (preceding the war-dance);

Pash-e-pa-ho expects now Nes-wa-ge, his friend, with his picked men—

Wanders delighted thy friend, aged chief, in the land of the spirits—

Stealthy as wild-cats, Da-ko-tas encompass the camp of the Delawares;

Three hundred grim-painted warriors, at sunrise loud-yelling assault it.

'Braves of Nes-wa-ge, we're dead men! but shall we die cravens?

Cried the Delaware chief when he saw the Da-ko-tas advancing.

Manfully fighting they fall. At the feet of the war-chief Four big Da-ko-tas lie dead, struck cold by his hatchet— Hatchets have wounded the oak whose mosses pillow the hero.

Deeply wounded by blows that were aimed at the face of Nes-wa-ge.

Slain twenty-six hated Siouxs by this brave and his comrades;

Twenty-three of the Del'wares lay mangled and dead on the hillside—

One only escaping—the tall grass concealed him retreating; Wounded and foot-sore, he brings the sad tidings to brave Pash-e-pa-ho.

Mad is the veteran—a fierce, driving whirlwind—a tempest of anger!

See him now lifted by braves to the back of his pony. The War-chief,

Stiffened' by age and rough service, no longer can mount unassisted;

Seated on horseback, not one of his braves can ride better.

Raising the war-whoop, he leads; the warriors dash to the river;

     Hastily painting their faces with mud, they spur through the water;
     Chasing the Siouxs, overtake them. Three hundred scalps the fresh trophy
     Th' Sauks and Mus-qua-kies returning exultant, exhibit.

Pash-E-Pa-Ho

Chapter One: In the Beginning

Sauk Wigwam

That same year, 1841, Captain James Allen erected a fort at the junction of the Raccoon and Des Moines rivers to keep peace among the Indians. It was first called "Raccoon Forks," but was soon renamed "Fort Des Moines."

The land that now forms Dallas County was ceded by the Sauk and Fox nation to the United States in a treaty signed on October 11, 1842. On January 13, 1846, the legislative body of the Indian Territory authorized creation of twelve new counties in the Iowa Territory. Dallas was one of them. The County was named for United States Vice President George M. Dallas, who served from 1845 to 1849. Later that same year, December 28, 1846, Iowa was admitted into the union as the 29th state.

In 1847, Dallas County residents voted to designate Penouch as the county seat. Penouch is an Indian name meaning "far away" (the name was changed to Adel in 1849). The county's population grew rapidly, with numerous settlers coming to claim homesteads.

Murder and Mayhem in Dallas County

The early pioneers of Dallas County were law-abiding and orderly citizens, intent on establishing and following the laws of the territory and the state of Iowa. They immediately set about putting in place all the necessary elements of a legal system, including a court system. The first session of the Dallas County District court was held on September 6, 1847. Since a proper courtroom had not yet been established, the session was held under a giant oak tree in the yard at the home of W. W. Miller, about two miles east of Adel. Judge James P. Charlton presided. The jury consisted of seventeen men, which was nearly all the voters in the county at that time.

Judge Charlton opened the session by declaring "They were prepared to take counsel together concerning the various breaches of law and order and heartless betrayals of trust which might be brought before them." They failed to find any cases to judge, however, and adjourned shortly after convening. All participants then retired to the front yard where they ate a big meal, prepared for them by the Millers, before making their way home. Jury duty had some perks, way back then.

The court, however, did issue one ruling at that session: There being no county seal, the court ordered that the eagle side of a 25-cent piece of American coin be the temporary seal of Dallas County until a proper one could be provided.

The situation of there being no cases for the first court session to adjudicate would not last for long. Like any growing area, the Dallas County Court System's officials would soon find that even a law-abiding citizenry would have its scoundrels and rascals.

One such scoundrel was the first settler of Spring Valley Township, a Hessian named "Dutch" Henry. Dutch settled, in the spring of 1848, west of the river and opposite of where Perry now stands, in a rather isolated homestead. His neighbors couldn't understand why he had chosen such an isolated place when homesteads closer to neighbors were available. When the neighbors came together for a cabin raising, Dutch Henry was among them. A stranger, who had just arrived from the east, saw Dutch Henry and thought he knew him.

Chapter One: In the Beginning

Approaching him with a smile, the stranger said "It strikes me sir that I have seen you before. Is not your name Henry Johns?"

"Nix, my name ish not dot, he ish von Dutch Henri, all der time, yaw," Dutch Henry replied. But after declaring himself not to be the man the stranger thought he was, Dutch Henry was suddenly (and strangely) stricken with violent intestinal pains. He lay face down in the grass until nightfall, writhing in pain but refusing any help. Then, in the darkness, Dutch Henry, or Henry Johns, slipped away and was never seen in Iowa again. The stranger was sure that the man was indeed Henry Johns who had stolen about $700 in Pennsylvania and escaped.

Horses were much needed but in short supply during this early time. Many immigrants came by foot or on stages, leaving any horses they might have owned behind. They hoped to purchase them in the new land but often found prices to be prohibitive. They resorted to using cattle and oxen to break the sod and till the soil. Because of this shortage, horses were often the target of horse thieves (what else would horse thieves target?). Gangs of horse thieves operated over a wide area and the few officers of the law available were unable to stop them. This situation soon led to the formation of vigilante committees whose actions were not limited to only horse thieves.

Another problem that the early settlers had to deal with was the "claim jumper," some of which had more ways to take your money than a roomful of lawyers. Once again, they resorted to vigilantism, but this time they gave their group a dignified name, "The Dallas County Claim Club."

Formed in 1848, the club prevailed upon Judge Burns to draft the bylaws to be carried out "without fear of the world, the flesh and the devil." He set about forming a three-man committee. This committee performed the duty thus assigned them, and reported through their chairman, Thomas Butler, the following by-laws which were accepted and adopted unanimously:

WHEREAS: Self-protection, the acquiring and peaceable possession of property are essential to the happiness and prosperity of the people; and
WHEREAS: Reckless claim jumpers, wolves in human form, are

prowling through the county for the purpose of robbing the settler of his claim and of the means of support; therefore, be it resolved,

1. That we pledge ourselves to protect every member of this club in his rights of claim, or against the pre-emption of adverse parties, without fear of the world, the flesh or the devil.
2. That no person shall be allowed to pre-empt, or to purchase from government any claim of a member of the club, without the unequivocal consent of the member.
3. That the filing of any intention to pre-empt, in contravention of the right of any member hereof, be regarded as an attempt to deprive one member of his rights under the eternal fitness of things, and we pledge ourselves one to another to meet the offender on the home stretch with logic of life or…
4. That a committee of three be raised, whose duty shall be to hear and adjust any disputes, evasions or disagreements that may arise with members of this club, or any case where claims of members are in dispute with outside, adverse claimants, of every character whatever.
5. That we pledge ourselves to sustain and uphold our committees and appointments in the performance of their several duties, and to enforce their decisions and adjudications to the very letter, with force and arms if necessary.
6. That a cordial invitation is hereby extended to every citizen of Dallas county to sign these articles of by-laws, and to assist in their faithful execution and enforcement.

Not enough laws had been passed by the governing bodies to cover every facet of civil matters, unlike today when we have about a dozen laws for every misdeed. So, the settlers sometimes had to execute their own laws. Fortunately, these were usually reliable and law-abiding citizens who desired only to punish those guilty of criminal activity.

The spring of 1850 was an exciting time for Dallas County and especially the residents of Adel. A mad rush had been sparked by the discovery of gold in California and everything seemed to be moving westward at a rapid pace. Greed was the motivation, and everyone struggled to get there before the others. The following is an eye-witness

Chapter One: In the Beginning

account: "It seems that bedlam itself had been let loose. A continuous line of wagons stretched away to the west as far as the eye could see. If a wagon was detained by being broke down, or by reason of a sick horse or ox, it was dropped out of line and the gap was closed up immediately. If a poor mortal should sicken and die, the corpse was buried hurriedly by the wayside, without a coffin or burial service. When night came on, the line of wagons was turned aside, and their proprietors would go into camp. Very soon, the sound of revelry would begin around the campfires thickly set on every hand, first to bottle and then to cards, to the echo of the most horrid oaths and imprecations that were ever conceived or uttered since the fall of man."

An article in the Des Moines Gazette, dated April 26, 1850, states the following: "The rush to California still continues with but little abatement. The number of teams that have crossed the Des Moines River, at this place, for the week past amount to 199 – with 540 men, making a total up to this time of 690 teams and 1,797 persons." So many Dallas County residents were pulling up stakes and heading west that the county had to elect three sheriffs in one year to replace the ones that were stricken by gold fever.

Since its beginning, the nation had struggled with the question of slavery. For years, as new land was added, especially by the Louisiana Purchase, a delicate balance was maintained between slave-holding and non-slave states. The Kansas-Nebraska Act, passed by the U.S. Congress on May 30, 1854, allowed people in the territories to decide for themselves whether to allow slavery within their borders. The Act served to repeal the Missouri Compromise of 1820, which prohibited slavery north of latitude 36°30′. The Kansas-Nebraska Act soon led to bitter fighting, especially in Kansas, to decide its status as a slave or free state.

Iowa was part of what was considered the north and had been admitted to the union as a free state. Dallas County, and much of Iowa at that time, was still considered part of the frontier. But it had never allowed slavery to exist within its borders, not even before Iowa became a state. Missouri was a slave state, however. Due to its location on the line between free and slave states, Iowa was an important part of the Underground Railroad which helped smuggle slaves to freedom. The route started from Tabor, in Fremont County, and crossed diagonally across Adair County, striking Summit Grove where Stuart is now located. From there, one line went east down what was known as Quaker Divide or Bear Creek area. The Bear Creek area began at a line going north from Dexter to the river and east to the Bilderback or Mitchell Mill on the South Raccoon. The other line crossed the Raccoon River near Redfield, then through Adel. Both lines came together at Des Moines, went on to Grinnell, then to Muscatine and up to Canada from there. It has never been determined how many slaves escaped through Dallas County on the Underground Railroad, but it was probably a considerable number

    Just because the fugitive slaves made it to Iowa didn't mean they were safe. Fugitive slaves had to be just as careful hiding in Iowa as they did in the South, due to slave hunters. Even in Iowa, if someone was caught harboring slaves they could be fined up to one thousand dollars and sentenced to six months in jail. But that didn't stop some Iowans.

    Many families took part in the Underground Railroad, but the Cook family was the most famous in Dallas County. They were Quakers and abolitionists. They made it their mission to house, protect, and transport fugitive slaves to their next stop on the trail. The Cook family transported many slaves from the Quaker Divide near Redfield to their next stop, usually the Des Moines area.

    The issue of slavery finally tore the country apart. On April 13, 1861, boonville Fort Sumpter was fired upon and a long, bitter and bloody war between North and South began. Iowa's sympathies were, for the most part, with the abolitionists and the Union.

    Once the rebellion began, Iowa Governor Samuel J. Kirkwood was called upon by the Lincoln Administration to provide one regiment of militia for immediate service. Kirkwood had doubts whether he could raise the 970 men that would be Iowa's quota. In only ten days, however, Iowa had raised not one but three regiments.

Chapter One: In the Beginning

    A great many brave men from Dallas County served in the Civil War. A number of them served with Sherman and marched with him through Georgia and the South. They came home from the war as changed men. No man can be involved in the kind of slaughter and destruction that the American Civil War created and not be changed forever. Most of these veterans resumed their previous occupations and lived peaceful lives. But there were those that were so affected by what they experienced that they would never be the same. Many of these rough and dangerous men moved west and helped create a period of lawlessness that romanticized the cowboys, gunslingers and lawmen portrayed in movies today. But not all of them went west, and Dallas County probably had its share of such men.

Chapter Two

John Bold

Along the Washington and Colfax Township line in north-central Dallas County is an area called "Panther." The Panther area is where many early settlers came, brought to this place by a stage line that ran north along the Raccoon River. Washington and Colfax Township's only post office, at that time, was at Panther. A German Baptist Church was organized there in 1869. At first, services were held in homes but four years later they built a large church building and called it the Panther Creek Church. A beautiful cemetery is located right west of the church. That early cemetery is the final resting place for the first victim of a murder committed in Dallas County.

It happened on a warm August day. John Bold had just finished bringing his cows in from the pasture and was preparing to do chores. The sound of cows bawling for their calves could be heard as Bold gathered up his stool and pail and prepared to do the milking. The few cows Bold owned were important to him. They provided milk to feed his family, manure to enrich his fields, meat for his table and the future prospect of developing a herd. Unknown to Bold, someone else had their eye on his cattle, and on Bold himself. Someone waiting in the shadows and out of sight.

As Bold went about his chores, he was still angry from the bitter quarrel he had that afternoon with his neighbor, J.E. Elliott. Elliott and Bold lived about three-quarters-of-a-mile north of Panther. Elliott lived on the west side of the road and Bold lived on the east. All that is known about the quarrel is that it concerned a cow. It may have been over a

Chapter Two: John Bold

calf that was born that spring to which both claimed ownership, but that is something we will never know.

Elliott was so angered by the bitter quarrel that he decided to take action against Bold. He went to another neighbor and asked to borrow a gun, claiming that Mrs. Elliot had fallen ill, and he was sure that some chicken soup would be just the thing to help cure her of her ailments. Elliott had no chickens of his own, but there was an ample supply of prairie chickens to be had for the taking. These birds freely roamed the prairie grasses back then, and all you needed was a gun and a good eye to put the magical curative power of chicken soup to work. This was not what Elliott had in mind, however.

Elliott was aware of Bold's choring habits and knew when he would be bringing his cows in from the pasture. After securing the shotgun, he made his way back to Bold's place. There, he hid and waited for Bold to return from the field with his cows. With a cold heart and evil intentions, Elliott took aim and pulled the trigger. In an instant, John Bold lay dying. He bravely lingered on for two days, however, before succumbing to his wounds. Dallas County, for the first time in its short history, had become the scene of a dastardly murder.

Although there were no telephones or automobiles in those early times, news of the shooting quickly reached Adel. As the news of the deed spread around the neighborhood, someone jumped onto a horse-drawn wagon and raced to town to notify sheriff A.W. Haines. Haines quickly mounted his horse and raced to the area to apprehend the shooter.

Meanwhile, Elliott ran two miles south to George Britton's place. He rapped on the door and when Britton appeared, he calmly explained to him what he had done. The two men talked over the situation and, as it was after dark by then, Elliott asked for a place to stay for the night. Britton agreed after Elliott assured him that he would turn himself in the next morning.

Meanwhile, Sheriff Haines began searching for Elliott. He went to a farm north of the Bold farm and searched a crawlspace under the house. Not finding Elliott, and with darkness hampering his search, the sheriff returned to town.

Elliot was true to his word, walking the three miles to town the next morning to give himself up.

Elliot was held for trial, but we don't know for sure just where. The County had voted, in 1861, to build a new jail but nothing further was done. There was talk of putting the jail in the second story of the courthouse, but that was deemed impractical. Finally, in 1871, the board of supervisors appropriated $5,000 for the purpose of building a two-story brick jail across the street north of the courthouse. Work was begun the following year, 1872, but whether it was completed by August 24th in time to accommodate Elliott as one if its first guests is unknown. In any case, he was held somewhere for trial.

Trial was held in the Dallas County Courthouse shortly after the incident. In spite of what appears to be overwhelming evidence, Elliott was acquitted of the murder charge. Maybe the jurors were ancestors of the O.J. Jurors.

John Bold is buried in the Panther Creek Church of the Brethren Cemetery. Bold's grave was the first one to be marked in Panther Creek Cemetery, but his was not the first burial there. His daughter, Martha Estella Bold, was buried in an unmarked grave after she died at the age of 5 on Feb. 29, 1871. When John Bold was buried next to his daughter, a marker was erected honoring both of them. Panther area folks will, hopefully, never let the legend of the shooting die. Although it was not the community's proudest hour, it was among its most memorable.

Chapter Two: John Bold

The gravestone reads: John N Bold Shot by J.E. Elliott Aug 23, died Aug 25, 1872

Chapter Three

The Unfortunate Case of Jasper Mason

Just a short four years after the John Bold incident, late in the summer of 1876, another dastardly murder occurred within the bounds of Dallas County. This time it happened in the southern part of the county near the small town of DeSoto. A young man named Jasper Mason was a passenger in a wagon traveling from Western Iowa to Des Moines. The driver, and owner of the wagon, was another young man known only by the name of Woods.

Born in Illinois in 1853 and left an orphan at an early age, Jasper Mason had worked on a farm until he was twenty years of age. That was when he came to Iowa. It is said that he had already acquired a roving disposition and a tendency to associate with disreputable characters. Late in the summer of 1876, he stopped at the town of Atlantic, Iowa, then a small hamlet in Cass county some 60 miles west of DeSoto. There he met Woods, who was travelling by wagon to Des Moines. An arrangement was made whereby Mason would go to Des Moines in company with Woods. They started together from Atlantic and made three stops on the way. The first stop they made was at Dexter, where they got some provisions. We may assume that these provisions included something to wash the road dust from their throats as they travelled the dusty primitive trails of the time. The next stopping place was at DeSoto, where they were noticed by a number of local

Chapter Three: The Unfortunate Case of Jasper Mason

residents. According to Mason's story, the two travelers had been drinking heavily and had been engaged in a prolonged and rather heated discussion of the respective merits of the then presidential candidates, Rutherford B. Hayes and Samuel J. Tilden. Apparently, politics were just as polarized back then as they are today.

At that time in our nation's history, the divisions caused by the Civil War were still very deep and could put some men in a horn-tossin' mood real quick. The issue of reconstruction served to keep those divisions at a boiling point. During the period following the American Civil War, from 1865 to 1877, the country was dealing with a multitude of problems. Among them, the aftermath of the Civil War's destruction, the transformation of the 11 former Confederate states back into the union as directed by Congress and making the newly freed slaves citizens with civil rights ostensibly guaranteed by three new constitutional amendments.

It was widely assumed, during the year 1875, that incumbent President Ulysses S. Grant would run for a third term as president. However, poor economic conditions, the numerous political scandals that had developed since he assumed office in 1869, and the first president George Washington's long-standing tradition of only two terms for holders of the highest office were reasons for him not to run. Grant's inner circle advised him to go for a third term, however, and he almost did. The House of Representatives had a different idea. They passed a resolution, by a vote of 233 to 18, that the two-term tradition would become law. Their intent was to prevent a dictatorship. Late in the year, President Grant ruled himself out of running in the election of 1876. He instead tried to persuade his Secretary of State, Hamilton Fish, to run for the presidency. But Fish declined, believing his 67 years made him too old for the role. Grant, nonetheless, sent a letter to the convention imploring them to nominate Fish. But somehow the letter was misplaced and never read out to the convention. Fish later confirmed that he would have declined the nomination, much like General Sherman (If nominated I will not run, if elected I will not serve), even had he been offered it.

When the Sixth Republican National Convention assembled in Cincinnati, Ohio, on June 14, 1876, it appeared that James G. Blaine would be the nominee. On the first ballot, Blaine was just 100 votes short of a majority. His vote began to slide after the second ballot, however, as many Republicans feared that Blaine could not win the general election. Anti-Blaine delegates could not agree on a candidate until Blaine's total rose to 41% on the sixth ballot. Leaders of the reform Republicans met privately and considered alternatives. They chose Ohio's reform governor, Rutherford B. Hayes. On the seventh ballot, Hayes was nominated with 384 votes to 351 for Blaine and 21 for Benjamin Bristow. William A. Wheeler was nominated for vice-president by a much larger margin (366–89) over his chief rival, Frederick Theodore Frelinghuysen, who later served as a member of the electoral commission that awarded the election to Hayes.

The Democrats held their convention, just nine days after the Republican convention, in St Louis, Missouri. This was the first political convention of any major party to be held west of the Mississippi River. New York Governor Samuel Tilden's battle against public corruption, along with his personal fortune and electoral success in the country's most populous state, made him an ideal candidate for the Democratic nomination for president in 1876. Tilden was selected on the second ballot. Tilden focused his campaign on civil service reform, support for the gold standard, and opposition to high taxes, but many of his supporters were more concerned with ending reconstruction in the South. The Democratic platform called for "immediate reform" of the federal government and, to forestall Republican charges of sectionalism, committed itself to the "permanence of the Federal Union." It also called for civil service reform and restrictions on Chinese immigration to the United States.

With all that going on, Woods and Mason would have had plenty to argue about. And as they continued "jugging and jawing," the argument became very heated as they both got tighter than bark on a log.

Chapter Three: The Unfortunate Case of Jasper Mason

The next stop for these two inebriated debaters was at a little grassy knoll just east of DeSoto, near where the road crosses Bulger creek. No one but Mason knows for sure what happened next, but he testified that near DeSoto the argument escalated into a "row." He claimed that Woods assaulted him with a knife and, believing his life was in danger, fired a revolver at Woods (from the grassy knoll?)

Although the team and wagon belonged to Woods, Mason traveled on alone after leaving Woods lying on the ground near death. Woods was found the next morning and taken to the home of Fon Van Meter. Here he lingered four days and died without making any statement as to the facts of the shooting. The attendant physician, Dr. A. J. Smith, convinced that the man had been murdered by his companion, began to do a little detective work. By making a number of inquiries, he managed to trace Mason to Prairie City, Iowa. Dallas County Sherriff J.W. Bly apprehended Mason at Prairie City and brought him back to Adel for trial. The people of DeSoto were clamoring for a swifter form of justice and had a rope ready if the culprit had been available to them.

The facts appeared that Woods had been murdered for his money and team, having apparently been shot as he lay under the wagon asleep. This created such a feeling at DeSoto that it was with the greatest difficulty that a lynching, in lieu of a trial, was prevented.

Mason was tried in the district court at Adel in October 1876. He was defended by T. R. North, an aspiring lawyer who would later become mayor of Adel and build the Adel Opera House. Mason claimed that he purchased the team and wagon, and therefore was not guilty of theft. The matter of the shooting was a case of self-defense. He also proclaimed that he felt no compunction in taking the team away, leaving his dying companion on the ground.

A peculiar feature of the law, at that time, was that the defendant in a criminal prosecution was not permitted to be a witness in his own behalf. The testimony of reputable citizens, who were familiar with the circumstances, was presented instead. After hearing only this testimony, the jury believed the accused was guilty of the crime as presented by the state. It seems a travesty of justice that one hundred years after the Declaration of Independence was signed, a defendant should be tried for murder where the evidence was all circumstantial and he is not allowed to testify in his own behalf. With no other witnesses, Mason was pronounced guilty and sentenced to life in prison.

Mason made repeated efforts for pardon but on account of protests from Dallas county people, who were convinced that justice demanded the full penalty to be paid, he was unsuccessful until 1907. That was the year he was finally able to get the sympathy of the legislature, who recommended a pardon. After 31 years as a guest of the State of Iowa at its prison facility in Anamosa, Governor Cummins granted him the pardon. Mason's pardon was probably also helped by a growing feeling that a man, convicted entirely upon circumstantial evidence, was not given justice.

Robert F. Woods said it this way in his book, "Past and Present of Dallas County, Iowa, Volume 1" When Mason stepped out of

Chapter Three: The Unfortunate Case of Jasper Mason

the doors of the Anamosa Prison, in April 1907, he closed a career of prison life exceeded by few prisoners in the United States. Coming out prematurely aged, his face lined with wrinkles, his body bent with labor, into a world that is entirely new and strange to him, it is little wonder that he seemed dazed and bewildered.

After gaining his freedom, Mason departed for South Dakota, where he expected to, once again, take up the profession of farming.

The accounts of some historical incidents don't always agree. In a book by Will Porter titled "Annals of Polk County, Iowa and the City of Des Moines" published in 1896, can be found the following story:

Munda Murder

There was a murder committed in 1876 in Dallas County, near the Polk County line. Jasper Mason, of Jasper County, was traveling with a man by the name of Martin Munda. One morning the dead body of Munda was found a short distance from the town of DeSoto. He had evidently been shot and killed. An inquest was held, and as it was known that Mason had been with the dead man in DeSoto and elsewhere, a search was made for Mason, who had suddenly disappeared. In a short time, he was found at his old home in or near Prairie City and was arrested. He was taken back to Dallas County, where he was almost immediately indicted for the murder of Munda. He was soon placed on trial and pleaded that he had killed Munda in self-defense after the latter had attacked him in a quarrel between the two. This defense was regarded as insufficient. Mason was found guilty and sentenced to imprisonment in the penitentiary at Fort Madison during life. There he was taken and has remained in confinement for nearly twenty years. At this writing he and his friends are making an effort to secure his pardon and a discharge from the penitentiary, where he has been serving so long a time.

This story certainly raises a few questions. Was it Martin Munda that was killed or a man named Woods? Was Jasper Mason sentenced to Fort Madison Prison or Anamosa Men's Reformatory? Will we ever know the answers to these pressing questions?

In the absence of any other evidence, I prefer to believe the Dallas County account rather than the Polk County version. Maybe I'm biased.

JASPER MASON HAPPY IN HIS DECLINING YEARS

Famous Ex-Convict, Wrongfully Imprisoned for Thirty-One Years, Now Prosperous in Oregon.

Word has just been received by the law firm of Heald & Linville from Dallas, Oreg., that Jasper Mason, who was released from the penitentiary at Anamosa about a year ago, having served thirty-one years of continuous confinement, and who was granted a pardon by the Thirty-second general assembly of Iowa through the instrumentality of F. A. Heald, his attorney, is meeting with a large measure of success in the world and is making good at his trade as an expert carpenter.

The Jasper Mason case will be remembered by the readers of The Gazette and the people generally. At the time of his release he had served thirty-one years in the penitentiaries of Iowa on a life sentence. Mr. Heald at the time was private secretary to the late Warden Hunter at Anamosa, became interested in the case of Jasper Mason, and devoted his time and energy to the prosecution of his case for a pardon. There were several interesting propositions of law in this

(Continued on Next Page)

Chapter Three: The Unfortunate Case of Jasper Mason

case which Mr. Heald raised before the legislature, and after a hard fight of nearly two years he was successful before both bodies of the legislature and the state authorities, and out of twenty-seven applications for pardons last winter at Des Moines Mr. Heald's case for Jasper Mason was the only successful one. Those who heard Mr. Heald's argument before the combined committees of the legislature in behalf of Jasper Mason pronounce it as one of the finest and most eloquent arguments and appeals ever heard in the legislative halls. With all of the prejudice and passion aroused in the state by the Busse and Cullen incidents which created a strong sentiment against all pardons, Mr. Heald was able to convince the legislators of Iowa that Jasper Mason should be pardoned.

Jasper Mason is making $5 per day as an expert carpenter and writes that he feels good for twenty-five years of active life yet to come. The life story of Jasper Mason reads like a romance and the record which he is making out of prison and after a lifetime of confinement behind prison walls, will demonstrate to his scores of friends all over the state who voted to set him free, that their judgment and confidence were not misplaced, but that it is only another illustration of what a regenerated and rehabilitated human life can do and what a man can accomplish if he has a chance and a true, loyal friend whose friendship has been the means of giving him an opportunity to make good.

Chapter Four

Adel's Most Exciting Day

It all began at approximately 8:45 on March 6, 1895, a cool and frosty morning. Smoke was slowly rising from the chimneys of most of the buildings around the courthouse square that morning. The merchants and tradesmen in the town of Adel were busy preparing for the day. Fires were stoked to take the chill off the late winter morning and most of the businessmen had already swept the wooden or concrete sidewalk in front of their establishments. Only a few horses were tied to the hitching posts this early in the morning. The crisp air smelled of many things, wood and coal burning in the heating stoves, grain being milled a few blocks away at the mill on the river and the odor of horse droppings, which was a familiar smell in the days before automobiles.

A buggy, being pulled by two horses...a black and a grey, had crossed the river at Ferry Street and was now turning north onto Vine Street. The two men in the buggy had followed the road along the North Raccoon River from the south, after staying overnight in a barn near Van Meter. The buggy they were riding in was commonly known as a top buggy. It had a folding canvas top, much like the early automobiles that would soon replace it. Although March is still winter in Iowa, the folding top was lowered, and its bows and canvas were folded behind the seat. The few citizens on the streets had no idea the two men in the

Chapter Four: Adel's Most Exciting Day

buggy were about to attempt something that would be remembered to this day in the history of Adel and Dallas County.

Although they were second cousins, the two men could not have been more different. The older of the two was a man named Orlando Poe Wilkin. Wilkin was born in Madison County to honest hardworking parents. Those parents, Mathew and Mary Wilkin, came to Iowa from Ohio before the Civil War. They settled on eighty acres in Crawford Township, Madison County near the town of Patterson. Mary, whose maiden name was Dougan, was born into a cattle-raising family. Some members of the Dougan clan were already ranchers in Wyoming and Montana.

Mathew Wilkin was a farmer and had served a short enlistment in the Civil War. His enlistment, in the First Iowa Cavalry, began on 5 September 1861. He was mustered out less than eight months later on 28 May 1862 at Butler Missouri. The First Iowa Cavalry was one of the first units to serve from Iowa. The soldiers provided their own horses, as the Union Army had not had time to set up procurement procedures and furnish the cavalry with government horses. Enlistments were for three years. The unit was sent to Missouri and had engaged in several battles before Mathew was mustered out. There is no record of a battle injury, but he probably suffered from consumption and was no longer fit to serve. Years later, Mary was able to obtain a soldier's pension for his service.

Mathew died of consumption (tuberculosis) September 5, 1869, leaving Mary a widow. The family, at the time of the 1870 census, consisted of: Mary Wilkin age thirty-seven, Jaun Fernado Wilkin age fourteen, Sonora Wilkin age ten, Orlando Poe Wilkin age six, Frontis (or Fronto) Wilkin age three, and Lucinda Wilkin age one. After the death of her husband, Mary sold their land in Iowa and moved her family to Montana, where she had close relatives. A newspaper article from the Daily Huronite of Huron, South Dakota, dated March 11, 1895, indicates that Orlando had a mother, sister and two brothers living near Livingston, Montana. The brothers referred to, though not named, would likely have been Juan and Frontis Wilkin. The newspaper states that the men were wealthy stock raisers.

Orlando chose a different path than his two brothers had chosen. Instead of raising cattle, he became a cattle rustler and thief, "wandering through Montana and the Northwest leading a life of vagabondage and crime," as the Huronite article states. The article also claims that Orlando was sent to the Montana State Prison at Deer Lodge, Montana. The specific charge and time he served could not be discovered, as Montana has not made these records available, if they still exist. Orlando Poe Wilkin is listed in the state census of Montana for the year 1891. He is shown as living in Helena, Montana, at Room 112 S. Benton Ave. and his occupation is "wiper"…Montana Central Railroad. A wiper is the man that cleans the rail cars after animals and other commodities are shipped in them. The Montana Central Railroad had become a part of the Great Northern Railway in 1889.

Orlando Poe Wilkin is next found in 1892 in the "Land of 1000 Lakes." Clay County, Minnesota is located along the western border of the state, just across the state line from Fargo, North Dakota. Moorhead, Minnesota is the largest city in the county and also the county seat. The Great Northern Railroad crosses Clay county and has been a part of its history for more than a century. It was in Clay County that Orlando, once again, ran afoul of the law. He received a four-year sentence for, as the newspapers of the time put it, "robbing a Jew of $700 worth of drafts." Grand Larceny was the official charge. The term "Jew," at that time may have referred to a travelling horse trader or merchant that did business by arguing prices.

The Minnesota State Prison is located in Stillwater, Minnesota near the Minnesota capital of St. Paul. It was built in 1850 to "house the state's rascals," and had served in that capacity for over 40 years by the time Orlando Poe Wilkin became an unwilling guest. Orlando began his sentence on January 27th, 1892 and was given the register number of 3387. He is listed on the register as "Ole" P. Wilkin, age 30, born in Iowa and admitted from Clay County, Minnesota. It is not surprising that a Minnesotan would change the name Orlando to "Ole," given the number of Scandinavian immigrants that settled there.

Orlando (or Ole) would serve his time with some famous outlaws who were also guests of Stillwater Prison. The two remaining

Chapter Four: Adel's Most Exciting Day

Younger brothers, of Missouri's famous James/Younger gang, had been residing within Stillwater's walls since 1876. Cole and James Younger had been sentenced after surviving the famous Northfield Minnesota bank robbery attempt. They would not be released until 1901. Another brother, Bob Younger, had died in Stillwater in 1889.

Prisoner Number 3387, "Ole" Wilkin, served his time and was released at the end of his sentence. He may have been punished for his crime, but he was not rehabilitated by any measure After his release from prison, Orlando went back to Patterson, Iowa rather than returning to Montana. He was not welcomed with open arms, however. Wilkin's uncle stated to the local newspaper that his family became afraid of Wilkin while he was stopping there, and that he considered him radically "off."

Charles Crawford, the young man that Wilkin recruited as his accomplice, stated that Wilkin was his second cousin and was related to all the Crawfords around Patterson. He also claimed that Wilkin had a mother living near Miles City, Montana. There was some difference in their ages, Wilkin being 32 and Crawford a young man of 19 years.

Wilkin, whose nickname was "Rowdy," was described as about 5 feet 8 inches tall, weighing 150 pounds, almost bald headed, light complexion, prominent cheek bones and with a four-week's growth of sandy beard. "He had the look of a desperate man," one person was said to have declared. Wilkin still wore the new set of clothes that he was given when he was set free from prison.

Charles W. Crawford also grew up near Patterson in Madison County. He did not have an easy childhood there. Born in 1875 to R.J. Crawford and Lucinda L. Stith, his father abandoned his mother before he was born. She took the child to live with an uncle, William W. Crawford, and worked out of the home to help provide for him. When he was about eight years old, his mother took him with her to Piedmont, North Dakota where she married J. E. Collins. In 1885, the family moved to Wyoming. Charles Crawford left his home in Wyoming at the age of twelve and "worked out." He returned to Iowa in 1892 and, once again, lived with his uncle, W. W. Crawford. Charles Crawford claimed to have had about two years schooling during his life, including the year in Winterset. "This was my life, up to the time that Orlando Poe Wilkin induced me to join him in crime," Crawford would later state. Crawford was described as 19 years old at the time, having a smooth round face and being taller and heavier than Wilkin. As one interviewer put it, "He talked freely as if he were telling the truth, but in his eye was a treacherous and deceitful look."

Wilkin had already proven himself to be a man who had little respect for the laws of a civil society. He had done his time with other men of like behavior and had learned at the hands of the masters in the world's best criminal training institution, prison. Wilkin's plan, if he had a plan, was to rob a bank and run like the blazes, hoping that nobody caught him. He had, no doubt, known bank robbers in prison who told him how it was done. He should have thought about how successful these mentors were, considering where they were presently residing. Did he think a team and buggy would outrun men on horseback for very long? Did he think he could escape the area by road, rail, or any other method, undetected? Did he think at all?

Crawford was reported to have been "loafing at Dexter (Iowa)" in the days before the robbery. Dexter, located in southwestern Dallas County, was known at the time for its harness racing. In fact, the town, after first being named Marshalltown, took its name from a famous harness racing horse. Before the turn of the century, there were three harness racing tracks in the Dexter area. This is probably what attracted young Crawford to Dexter.

Crawford was a young man who had yet to find a purpose in life. He was apparently easily influenced, and when Wilkin offered him a chance at adventure and riches, he went along, although somewhat reluctantly it seems. Neither man had strong ties to the things that civilize men such as a job, family or faith.

Wilkin had spent a few days in Winterset before the robbery, where he was observed in front of the Citizen's Bank looking in the window, "as if he were sizing it up and taking bearings." It's no surprise, however, that Winterset was not chosen as the target of their plan, considering their faces were known in that town.

Chapter Four: Adel's Most Exciting Day

The robbery scheme was apparently hatched at the home of Wilkin's uncle, William W. Crawford of Patterson, but without his knowledge. On Sunday, Wilkin borrowed a team and buggy from his Uncle Crawford, saying he wanted to go over toward Wick to visit a young woman. Wick is a small settlement in Warren County, just south of present Martinsdale, and approximately ten miles from Patterson. Wilkin promised to have the buggy back by Monday morning, a promise he had no intention of keeping.

An interesting note, in a newspaper report, states the following: "A letter was found in Wilkin's pocket addressed to Lander Wilkins, Patterson, Madison Co. Iowa. It was on the strength of this letter that he borrowed the buggy." Was this a letter from the young lady at Wick? Unfortunately, this is probably all we will ever know about this letter.

Wilkin somehow obtained a Spencer slide action repeating shotgun. If it was borrowed from his uncle, the one who provided the buggy, it would be interesting to know how he explained also needing a shotgun to go visit a young lady?

The Spencer Model 1882 Repeating Shotgun, that Wilkin borrowed, was the first slide action shotgun on the market. It was based on Spencer's celebrated breech-loading rifle of Civil War fame. The shotgun held six rounds and was available in 12 and 10 gauge. It was usually a reliable firearm. Usually.

Crawford claims that he met Wilkin on Sunday. Wilkin was traveling with the team and buggy and Crawford was on horseback. Wilkin asked him to go along with him. When Crawford asked, "What for?" Wilkin said he would tell him later. Rather than joining him in the buggy, Crawford remained on horseback and followed along with Wilkin. They stayed overnight Sunday with a farmer near Indianola. The next morning, Monday, they entered Indianola, a town of 3,000 population at that time, and the county seat of Warren County. Wilkin wanted to "go through" the bank as he put it, but Crawford objected, claiming that he had an aunt living in Indianola who might recognize him. Wilkin was unable to persuade the reluctant young man to join him. The aunt mentioned by Crawford was probably Mrs. George Wright, wife of a former pastor of the Methodist Episcopal Church of Indianola.

Not having accomplished their objective in Indianola, they went north to the little settlement of Summerset. There they spent Monday afternoon and night at a boarding house. Wilkin wanted to rob, or as he again put it, "go through," a grocery store in Summerset. Crawford's reluctance, once again, defeated that project.

Tuesday morning, they traveled to Norwalk where, for some unknown reason, Crawford left his horse with Mrs. Cash Small and got in the buggy with Wilkin. It's not known who this Mrs. Cash Small was. Perhaps the horse became lame or was wore out. If that wasn't the case, Crawford would have had a much better chance of escaping, after their planned robbery, if he had stayed on horseback.

Norwalk was a small town of less than three hundred population at the time. It is located in Warren County near the Polk/Warren County line. Norwalk was a prosperous town and had an established bank. Wilkin thought he had found his bank and was anxious to "go through" it. Crawford was again reluctant, however.

Wilkin had had just about enough of the young man's "lack of nerve," but was unable to change his mind. When they left, Wilkin said they might have got $5000 at Norwalk. Crawford did not say if it was another aunt living in Norwalk or just what it was that caused his reluctance.

Des Moines was a short distance to the north of Norwalk but was probably not a good place for a beginning and untested bank robbery duo. Des Moines had a full-time police force. They decided to seek the right bank by heading west. The next town to be honored with a visit from the "would be" robbers was Cumming.

Chapter Four: Adel's Most Exciting Day

Cumming had been incorporated in 1886 and sat along the Chicago, St. Paul & Kansas City Railroad. It consisted of 14 blocks and 125 surveyed lots. Cumming had a restaurant but did not yet have a bank. They made their plans to head on west while taking dinner in Cumming. Wilkin was still convinced that somewhere nearby there was a town with a bank they could "go through."

The two-man gang left Cumming with both now riding in the little buggy being pulled by a two-horse team. They were five or six miles southeast of Adel, and about halfway between DeSoto and Van Meter, when they stopped for the night. A farmer named Hester, who could not have known their intentions, gave them space in his barn for the night. The horses needed feed and rest and the men needed shelter. It was early March and still winter. Unless March came in like a lamb that year, temperatures were probably around the freezing mark or below. Wilkin and Crawford had been on the road for three days and had traveled approximately 70 miles. So far, they had nothing to show for their efforts. The next day would not be as uneventful.

"There's our bank," Wilkin told Crawford as they passed the Adel State Bank, after arriving in town. The two-story building still stands on the west side of the courthouse in about the middle of the block. It is one of the most ornate buildings in Adel's downtown. Wilkin must have thought, from the prosperous look of the bank and the town, that this would be a rewarding target.

Wilkin was not in the mood for any more excuses from Crawford. He threatened him that he must go with him this time or he would turn the shotgun on him. Wilkin must have been convincing as Crawford did not bring up an aunt, or any other relative in Adel who might recognize him, and reluctantly went along with the plan.

They drove on south on the dirt street past the bank to the corner of Court and Vine (9th Street) and tied their team to the rack north of the restaurant. "How's your nerve?" Wilkin asked Crawford as he loaded the shotgun.

"Not very good," Crawford admitted.

With Wilkin carrying the shotgun under his coat and Crawford carrying a cloth grain sack to put all the money in, they walked the half block back down Vine St. to the bank.

Joseph Fair had been in the bank early and had done some business with Mr. Leach, the cashier. As he concluded his business, Mr. C. D. Bailey, a town merchant, came in the bank. Mr. Fair took the opportunity to pay Bailey some money he had owed him. As Fair left the bank, he was met at the door by Wilkin and Crawford.

Bailey was standing at the desk on the south side of the room when the two strangers walked in. He observed the younger man step up to the cashier's desk and say something to Mr. Leach. "I do not think Mr. Leach understood him," Bailey would later testify.

Leach had just opened the vault and was ready to carry the money for the day's business to the counter. There was a small sack of money already on the counter. The time, registered by the Thompson's Regulator on the wall, was 8:50 a.m.

"I want to make a deposit," Crawford told Leach. Leach replied that he would wait on him in a minute. Wilkin then said something to Crawford, who turned and looked at him. Wilkin then told Leach to "Fill up the sack and be quick about it." Leach supposed that he was addressing his remarks to the younger man instead of him, according to Bailey.

When Leach hesitated, after Wilkin made his demand to fill the sack, Wilkin opened fire. Leach estimated that he was three or four feet away from the barrel of the shotgun when he was struck in the left shoulder. Wilkin then turned and shot Bailey, hitting him under the chin and on the top of his left shoulder. As Bailey was falling to the floor, Wilkin quickly worked the slide of the shotgun and fired again. This shot perforated Bailey's neck, exposed the jawbone, and about annihilated his collar, tie and shirt bosom.

Chapter Four: Adel's Most Exciting Day

Crawford then came around Wilkin, who had moved in front of him, and kicked in the small door at the end of the counter. He came in behind it where Leach, and the vault were. Leach, although badly wounded, got up and threw the money back in the safe before Crawford could grab it. He closed the door just as Wilkin fired another shot at him. Most of this shot missed Leach and hit the stove behind him. Crawford grabbed what money was left on the counter and put it in the sack. The money in the sack amounted to $272.30.

George Clarke, a young Adel attorney, had an office above the bank with his partner, John B. White. The stairs to his office were in the attached building to the south of the Adel State Bank building. There was a short hallway at the bottom of these steps. Clarke heard the four shots and immediately ran down the steps and through the hallway to the sidewalk. In his excitement, he tried to enter the bank without first opening the door. When he did open the door part way, Wilkin shoved the shotgun into his chest and pulled the trigger. The shell either failed to fire or Wilkin had not chambered a new shell after his last shot. Clarke didn't wait to find out. He immediately left and ran back up the steps faster than he had come down them.

Thomas J. Deaton, a local carpenter, was close by and heard someone say there was a crazy man in the bank who had shot the cashier. Deaton ran to the bank, stepped up on the concrete steps and reached towards the door. A man inside the bank pointed a shotgun at him and Deaton immediately backed off. "I got back out of the road," he later explained.

Sheriff Payne happened to be in Lea Thorton's Drug Store, the next building north of the bank, when the shots were heard. Payne had his revolver with him. The robbers, by now, had decided it was time to exit and were standing in the doorway of the bank preparing to make their get-away. Sheriff Payne drew his revolver and fired at them, missing but forcing them back into the bank. As Payne started to follow them into the bank, Wilkin turned and fired at the sheriff. Fortunately, the shot went wide of the mark. Payne's revolver would not work after the first shot and he stepped into the hall that led to the steps up to Clark's office and attempted to fix it. That was the opportunity the robbers needed to escape. This time they exited the back door of the bank, which led into the alley.

By now, everyone within earshot was aware that something was going on. Men grabbed whatever guns they could put their hands on and headed for the bank.

Wilkin acted as if he was no longer in control of his senses. He randomly fired at everyone in sight as he and Crawford ran for the buggy. It was a scene reminiscent of a Wild West movie.

Hearing the shots, J. M. Byers and Cecil Decker ran down the stairway into the alley south of Thornton's. No sooner had they appeared in sight than they received a charge of shot. Wilkin also fired across the square at J. L. Simcoke, who was unlucky enough to receive some stray shot. Postmaster Barr stepped out in front of the post office to see what was going on. The robbers, who were going toward him, yelled "Get back there!" and fired at him. He got back quick enough to avoid most of the buckshot.

Clerk of Court Anthony M. McCall was in his office in the courthouse and had watched the origin of the trouble. He ran from his office to Blanchard's Hardware, grabbed a 10-gauge shotgun and several 12-gauge shells, bravely intending to halt the robbers. He overtook the two fleeing robbers just as they reached their buggy at Vine and Court. Pointing the gun at them, he demanded they give up. Wilkin, having already shot several men, had no hesitation in adding to the day's total. He quickly raised his shotgun and fired at the brave clerk. When he squeezed the trigger, however, nothing happened. A shotgun will not fire when there is no shell in the chamber. Thinking he had the best of the match, McCall leveled the barrel of his shotgun

Chapter Four: Adel's Most Exciting Day

and pulled the trigger. Again, nothing happened. A 12-gauge shell will not fire in a 10-gauge shotgun. The standoff ended in a draw.

As Crawford untied the horses, Wilkin kept guard with his empty shotgun. Newspaper editor Wagner, who lived across the street and had heard the noise, stepped out of his house. He was greeted by the sight of a shotgun pointed at him. "Get the Hell back in the house," the man holding the shotgun demanded. Wagner asked no questions and quickly complied.

The two robbers jumped in the buggy and whipped the horses into action. The chase was on! Crawford furiously lashed the horses with the reins as Wilkin shoved shells into the shotgun. They headed west on Court street past the schoolhouse and up the hill toward the brick and tile works. Men on horseback were after them before they even passed the schoolhouse, which was only two blocks up Court street.

The shootout on the street resulted in four more citizens being injured, but none as badly as Leach and Bailey. Robert S. Barr, 57-year-old postmaster of Adel, was hit in the head and wrist. James L. Simcoke, a 35-year-old insurance agent, received a slight wound in his neck. John M. Byers, 65, who had served as Dallas County Sheriff twenty years earlier, was shot in the hand. Cecil Decker, a 17-year-old boy, was hit in the head and arm. Fortunately, none of these injuries proved serious.

Windows in Miss Garoutte's millinery store and Verne Russell's restaurant were broken by stray shots, but there was no other physical damage reported.

Men quickly scrambled to form a posse and join in the pursuit of the two robbers. The extent of injuries of Leach and Bailey were not known yet, so the posse assumed that the two men had been fatally injured and that the men they were chasing were not just robbers but murderers. Guns were loaded and all the serviceable horses at Colonel McCoy's livery stable, at 10th and Main, were saddled.

The robbers, after reaching the end of Court Street, made a one-block jog south to Main St. They followed the road west, then turned south, crossed the railroad tracks just past the brick and tile works and then turned west again. This road, known at that time as the Redfield Road, angled to the south slightly as it continued west. Three men were now in close pursuit on horseback, Den Snyder, Charley Warford and Tom Reynolds. They stayed close but never any closer than the range of the 12-gauge shotgun that Wilkin was threatening them with.

As they left the town of Adel on their wild buggy ride, Wilkin took the sack of money and removed four dollars. "We'll need to buy some more shells," he told Crawford. Wilkin must have still had some optimism for a better outcome than what they appeared to be heading for.

When they got to the Kissick place, two-and-one-half miles west of town, the robbers turned south on a dirt road (now county P-58 approximately) leading toward the South Raccoon River. As they passed the farms on this wild chase, Snyder yelled out to all the farmers along the way to grab their guns and help with the pursuit. Charles Kissick, a young farmer living at the corner of the Redfield road and the dirt road going south, and apparently a good shot with a Winchester rifle, joined in the chase.

Roads, at that time, were nothing like they are today. At best, they were little more than wide paths through the fields and timbers. They were not graded or graveled. These roads were all but impassable after a rain, due to the mud, and were rutted and rough even when they were dry.

The chase continued south approximately two miles to a "T" intersection where a little country church sat on the northeast corner. This road is now 330th St. and the church has been gone for many years. The fleeing robbers turned east on this road and followed it about

Chapter Four: Adel's Most Exciting Day

one mile. Just past the Burke Garoutte farmhouse, they turned south again. This is where their wild journey would end.

This road, now nothing more than a narrow lane, led to the banks of the South Raccoon River. The road went south from the main road and then made a sharp turn to the west as it approached the river. At that time there was a low water river crossing, or ford, at the end of the road, known as O'Neal's Crossing. The Henry Harrison O'Neal farmstead and the crossing were on the short east/west part of the road.

As they raced towards the river, Charles Kissick took careful aim at where he thought one of the robbers would be sitting in the buggy. He was unable to see them, due to the folded top of the buggy being directly behind them, blocking his view. He fired his rifle but did not hit a robber. The bullet, however, crashed through the buggy top and wounded one of the horses. The wounded animal made the team unmanageable and one of the buggy wheels struck a log as they attempted to turn west toward the river. The buggy upset, throwing both Wilkin and Crawford out on the ground.

Crawford ran toward the trees and brush along the river and crawled under a brush pile. He might have thought it a good hiding place, but he was quickly proved wrong. His pursuers soon spotted him. Thinking that further resistance was futile, he put his hands in the air and surrendered. Crawford would find out later that his captors were all unarmed.

Wilkin sat down by the overturned buggy and reloaded his shotgun. He then got up and started down the road on foot, stopping every few steps to turn and point the gun at the growing posse. When he reached a small barn that was part of the farmstead, he ran in and began firing at the posse from inside. They returned fire while calling for him to come out and surrender. In spite of what was said to be hundreds of shots fired into the barn, Wilkin remained defiant.

Crawford's captors used a hitching strap to bind his arms and then brought him to the barn where all the action was taking place. He offered no resistance, fearing that a nearby tree and a rope might serve the posse's desire for a lynching if he became too much trouble.

By now, the telegraph wire had alerted the nearby towns of Redfield, DeSoto and Dallas Center. Men from these places started arriving to add their firepower to an already one-sided battle.

Sheriff Payne grabbed Crawford and used him as a shield to approach the barn with a demand for an immediate surrender. When Wilkin did not answer, Crawford cried out, "Harvey, come out and give yourself up." There was still no response. Crawford then dropped the phony alias and called Wilkin by his real name, pleading for him to give up. That brought a reply from inside the barn. Wilkin angrily shouted that not only would he rather die than give up, if he had another load in his gun, he would kill Crawford as well.

Wilkin probably was out of ammunition by this time, but the sheriff could not be sure of this. It was discovered later that the only money missing from the sack of coins and silver was the $4 that Wilkin took out to purchase more shells. In his statement to F. M. Hoeye, Crawford said they only had 12 shells to start with.

Seeing that a peaceable end to this conflict did not seem forthcoming, Sheriff Payne decided on a different tact. He ordered that a pail of kerosene be brought forth and handed it to Crawford, who by now was pleading pitifully for Wilkin to give up. The sheriff directed Crawford to splash the kerosene on the pile of hay and fodder next to the barn and set it ablaze (the record indicates nothing about the owner of the barn being given a vote in this plan). Crawford now had a difficult decision to make. If he didn't obey, the crowd was in a mood to lynch him on the spot and Sheriff Payne might be powerless to stop them. If he went forth toward the barn as directed, his partner might make good on his promise and shoot him, especially considering his purpose in approaching the barn. Crawford decided that the sheriff's plan offered better prospects than the angry men surrounding him. With

Chapter Four: Adel's Most Exciting Day

the pail of kerosene and matches in hand, he moved toward the barn. Wilkin probably did not have "another load in his gun" as he did not make good on his threat to kill Crawford.

The pile of straw was set ablaze and soon the dry boards of the barn smoked and smoldered and burst into flames. Wilkin remained in the burning inferno as long as he could. With blistered face and singed hair and beard, Wilkin finally leapt from the fires of hell like a wild animal. He was met by cries of, "Throw up your hands." Rather than comply, Wilkin instinctively turned back toward the flames and appeared to consider leaping back in. His whole being repelled at that idea and he turned and looked as if he might try to run.

Sheriff Payne was powerless to stop what happened next. A farmer named Pritchard was said to be the first to fire upon the singed and smoldering villain. His shot was followed by the reports of many rifles and revolvers as bullets plowed into Wilkin's body from every direction. Those without guns hurled stones and sticks at the now prostrate body. Later examination revealed that there were several wounds in the body. Two wounds to the head and one in the side were deemed the fatal shots.

With one of the robbers dealt with, the mob turned their attention toward the other member of this duo, with an eye towards suspending him from the end of a rope. Fortunately, Crawford was nowhere to be found. While the angry mob's attention was on Wilkin, Sheriff Payne had hurried Crawford away from the scene. They were, by then, well on their way to Adel.

Some of the more rational men loaded the body of the dead robber into a butcher's wagon owned by Reynolds and Utz, the local butcher shop. Others searched the route that the desperate robbers had followed and were able to find the money taken in the robbery. The money, all $272.30 minus the $4 that Wilkin had optimistically removed for the future purchase of ammunition, was returned to the bank at 10:45 a.m. that same morning by Sheriff Payne. Just one hour and 55 minutes had passed from the time the first shot was fired in the bank building. In that short amount of time, one robber was dead, one robber was in jail and the money was back in the bank.

T. J. Deaton, in his statement to the grand jury, relates that he asked Crawford what they did with the little iron tray that was on the counter at the bank, which the robbers had taken. "He told me that it was out west of the schoolhouse (Adams No. 5) on the north side of the ditch. Afterwards I went out and found it where he told me it was," Deaton stated.

When Wilkin's battered and well-ventilated body was taken into town, people crowded around to get a glimpse. "You can't handle him too rough," someone hollered as they took the body from the wagon. "Drag him on the ground like a hog," and many similar remarks were also heard. The body was propped up in a chair in front of the bank as a grizzly reminder that crime did not pay. Seeing the body displayed in such a manner did little to calm the angry feelings the citizens held toward the surviving robber.

Sheriff Payne was able to reach town with his prisoner ahead of the angry mob and now had his hands full. Crowds began appearing in town from all directions, demanding a lynching. The armory at Perry was emptied of firearms and a large group from that vicinity was among the crowd demanding a lynching. Several members of the angry crowd carried ropes.

Lynching, as well as legally sanctioned hanging, was a seldom used remedy for lawlessness in the state of Iowa. Never-the-less, there are several cases of hangings and mob lynching in Iowa's early history. The earliest recorded incident of justice at the end of a rope happened in Burlington on June 25, 1845. John Miller, an old German, was murdered in his home on Devil Creek in Lee County. William and Stephen Hodges were arrested for the crime at Nauvoo, a Mormon city. A jury found them both guilty and sentenced them to death.

Chapter Four: Adel's Most Exciting Day

A small gallows was immediately built. Muffled drums and a dirge played by a brass band led the lumber wagon that carried the young men, sitting on their coffins, to their date with destiny. People gathered at the scene, even bringing their young children to witness the event.

As they stood on the gallows, William Hodges remained silent, but Stephen screamed out, "You are putting two innocent men to death. Hang us if you will. We are Mormons!"

A silence pervaded the crowd. Sheriff McKinney loathed doing the hanging and desperately searched for a way out of the terrible duty. He held up the hatchet that would cut the rope holding the platform that the men stood on. Severing it would send them to their deaths. Facing the crowd, he called out "I will give any man $50 to cut this rope."

$50 was a fortune in the 1840's, but not enough to entice any volunteers. With no other choice, the reluctant sheriff finally held up the hatchet and counted "once, twice, thrice," and brought the hatchet down, cutting the rope.

1857 was the worst year in Iowa's early history for vigilante justice. At least sixteen men had their necks stretched in Jackson, Jones, Cedar and Clinton counties alone. The extrajudicial vigilance committees, or "Regulators" as they were sometimes called, rode in broad daylight and dealt rough justice to the rascals and scoundrels of that area. Not one member of this mob of hangmen ever suffered conviction or imprisonment, as public sentiment generally favored them. Anger over 15 unsolved murder cases, in Jackson County alone, helped fuel the righteous indignation of the mob. The year 1857 laid bare just how thin a line exists between the rule of law and the rope, due process and mob rule. Even before the "wild west" became associated with rough justice, there were mob hangings in Iowa.

The Regulators stormed jails and hanged men without trial, or evidence, and even threatened county officials that they thought derelict in their duty. They even insinuated themselves into issues of property taxes and boundaries. By this time in Iowa's history, the court systems were operating, and county sheriffs were in office to enforce the law. However, frustration with continuances and changes of venue and all the other encumbrances of our court system, angered county residents. Mob rule took over when they saw murderers and horse thieves walking away free men.

At one point in 1857, with a lynch mob of over 200 men outside the stone jailhouse in the town of Andrew in Jackson County, Sheriff Foley barricaded himself, along with his prisoner, in the top floor of the jail. He waited there with pistols cocked, ready for anyone who would challenge him. Not even the mob leaders dared face what waited at the top of the stairs.

Another incident occurred, just three years later, in the town of Fairfield. A feeble old man by the name of Kephart was accused of the murder of several members of a family in nearby Batavia. A mob of over 250 men stormed the jail where he was being held and took him to the gallows that they had erected. The men, who were said to be respected citizens of the community, had already dug Kephart's grave by the time they witnessed him stretching the rope.

Hiram Wilson was another Iowan whose evil deeds brought him the opportunity to swing from the end of a rope. It happened on July 6, 1870 in Lucas County, when the sheriff attempted to arrest Wilson. According to newspaper accounts from 1870, Sheriff Gaylord Lyman led Hiram Wilson out the door of a Chariton saloon in the rear of a building and walked him toward the courthouse. Wilson turned and pulled a pistol. The older sheriff was apparently unmoved by the young man's threat and stepped toward him to take him back into custody. The young man pulled the trigger, shooting Sheriff Lyman in the belly. "You have killed me," Lyman said to the young man. Citizens took the law into their own hands and young Hiram Wilson was lynched.

Chapter Four: Adel's Most Exciting Day

From 1882 to 1968 there were nineteen recorded lynchings in Iowa. Seventeen of the nineteen were of white men and only two were of black men. Sheriff Payne's brave actions saved Charles Crawford from being added to that statistic. He was able to cool the situation a bit when he bravely stood before what was quickly becoming a lynch mob and proclaimed that he would defend the prisoner with his life.

Unsure of his ability to hold off the crowd until cooler heads prevailed, Sheriff Payne asked his friend F. M. Hoeye, the owner of the Perry Daily Chief newspaper who was in town reporting on the story, to take a statement from Crawford as to his part in the robbery. Payne wanted to prepare, as much as possible, for the death of the 19-year-old robber if the crowd could not be controlled. As Hoeye was taking the statement in the jail cell, the crowd managed to get to the window and hurl sticks and stones at the prisoner. Even an occasional gun barrel appeared but was quickly swatted away by the brave men Payne had recruited to watch the outside of the jail.

Things got even worse as evening approached. A large group of mounted men, who had arrived from the west part of the county, announced that they were there to hang the prisoner.

It was only after the doctors announced that none of the injuries suffered by the citizens that day would be fatal, did calm return. The angry mobs started to disperse. Sheriff Payne, and those brave men who assisted him, had saved Crawford from vigilante justice at the end of a rope.

The news of the robbery quickly spread. As far away as New York and California, newspapers carried the story of the bank robbery. It was a time when bank robberies were not that common and a daring hold-up in a little town in Iowa, with a chase and a shoot-out, made for interesting reading.

A good example of the type of coverage was the Atlanta Constitution of Atlanta, Georgia. This is the paper that Dr. Caldwell, one of the owners of the bank, was reading on the railroad car while vacationing in the south and first learned of the robbery of his bank. The story caption read: *The funds of the bank were saved by the presence of mind of the cashier, who, after receiving a load of lead in his body, swung shut the door to the vault and turned the combination.* The sensationalized account caused Caldwell to cut his winter vacation short and leave immediately for home.

The most accurate account of the events that day appeared in the Perry (Iowa) *Daily Chief* the following day, March 7, 1895. F. M. Hoeye, the reporter for the story, had worked for several newspapers in Dallas County, both as a reporter news gatherer and owner, and had just recently purchased the *Perry Daily Chief*. He learned of the robbery at 9 a.m. that morning, as the chase was still in progress. He left immediately for Adel, where he spent the day interviewing people and gathering facts. His account matches the actual testimony of witnesses, who were under oath, and other facts that could be verified. When Sheriff Payne was concerned that he might not be able to hold off the angry mob who wanted to take Crawford from the jail and lynch him, he asked his friend, F. M. Hoeye, to go to the jail and get all the information he could from Crawford. Payne trusted him to get the facts and knew he would have an accurate account if something happened to his prisoner.

The story that Hoeye was able to put together appeared on page two of the paper and was billed as a later and more accurate version than the story on page one. The earlier story on page one was just as inaccurate as the stories in most of the other papers. Following are some of the headlines that appeared in the papers:

Chapter Four: Adel's Most Exciting Day

The Perry Daily Chief

A TERRIBLE CRIME
Two Men Attempt to Rob the Adel State Bank
Cashier Leach Narrowly Escapes Being Murdered
SIX CITIZENS WOUNDED
C.D. Bailey was in the Bank and is Dangerously Wounded Twice, also Decker, Byers, Barr and Simcoke
Only Three Hundred Dollars were taken and it was all Recovered Except Four Dollars
DALLAS COUNTY IN ARMS
Possess Organized in all Sections--Robbers are Followed and Captured Seven Miles Southwest of Adel
Crawford Surrenders, Wilkin is Burned Out of his Hiding Place and Killed --Both from Madison County
ONE AN EX-CONVICT, THE OTHER ONE AN AMATUER
They Had Planned to Rob an Indianola Bank last Monday but gave it up and came to Adel
Sheriff Payne Does Good Work in Protecting the 19-year old Criminal--The Surviving Robber Interviewed

The Atlanta Constitution

BANK ROBBERS SHOT
Two Farmers Make an Attempt to Clear Out a Bank
FOILED BY A BRAVE CASHIER
They Scoop Some Silver in a Bag and Run
HOT PURSUIT GIVEN BY CITIZENS
A Battle Kept Up for Twelve Miles--A Barn is Fired and the Fugitive is Killed as He Escapes.

The Winterset Madisonian

BANK ROBBERY AT ADEL
Two Madison County Young Men, Orlando Wilkin and C. W. Crawford, Of Patterson, Engage in Bank Robbery in a Daring but Bungling Way

The New York times

BANK ROBBER SHOT DOWN
A MOB THREATENS LYNCHING FOR HIS CAPTURED COMPANION
SEVERAL CITIZENS WERE WOUNDED

For one newspaper, the timing of the robbery could not have been worse. *The Dallas County News*, a weekly paper delivered on Wednesdays, was one of the two local papers. Since the robbery occurred on Wednesday and the paper was mostly printed, they could not get a new version out in time.

"The News had one side of its issue printed last week before the bank robbery occurred and therefore unable to even print half sheets for extras. Its edition was exhausted long before the call for papers was satisfied."

The following Wednesday's edition of *the Dallas County News* for March 13 had news of the robbery under the heading "Bank Robbery Notes." Following are some interesting paragraphs:

Col. McCoy furnished fourteen head of horses last Wednesday to be used in the race after the bank robbers.

Chapter Four: Adel's Most Exciting Day

Press representatives were here last Wednesday from Des Moines, Guthrie Center, Dallas Center and Perry gathering items regarding the bank robbery.

The Chicago Record says Adel is built of the right kind of stuff, has sand in her craw and is alright generally, without any of Chicago's boodle officers.

Postmaster Barr, while his wrist was being probed for extra shot, said that he usually liked to argue a given proposition but the robber's suggestion to step aside was an exception.

We wish to swear to the falsity of the statement which went the rounds of the press to the effect that several shots were fired into Wilkin's body after he fell dead in front of the barn. Not a shot was fired after the first volley.

In the chase after the bank robbers last week, Den Snyder had a bad backside. For a few days afterward he inclined upon a feather cushion on his chair. Otherwise he took his meals standing. Charley Warford had a similar experience.

Mr. Frank P. Clarkson of the Register was a welcome visitor at this office last Wednesday, being here in the interest of that paper in reporting the exciting events of that day.

W. B. McLinn came up from Des Moines last Wednesday to take Mr. Leach's place in the bank for a few days. He was formerly assistant cashier of the bank and therefore able to drop at once right into the work.

The board of Supervisors will be asked to pay for the barn and corn burned last week in dislodging Wilkin, the bank robber, from his hiding place. The burning of the barn was necessary and was done in an effort to capture a criminal. We think the county ought to and will pay the bill.

In saying that we are glad that one of the bank robbers was shot and killed last Wednesday, and that no mob violence was done to the other after he surrendered, we think we voice the sentiment of this whole community. All would have been glad if both had a chance to surrender. The effect would have been healthy.

Adel's other local paper, *The Dallas County News,* competitor to *The Dallas County Record,* was more fortunate, as their paper was delivered on Friday. The entire front page and much of the last page, of the Friday March 8 edition, was devoted to the story of the robbery. They even published two pictures of Wilkin's body as it was displayed to the coroner's jury and to the citizens on the sidewalk in front of the bank. They had time to get the story fairly accurate as to the main details. Some of the local citizens that they interviewed, however, may have enhanced their role in the story just a bit.

An interesting article appeared in the *St. Louis Post-Dispatch* on Monday March 11, 1895. The headline was "**The Boy Bank Robber - Charles W. Crawford tells His Early History."** Included in the short article is a drawing purporting to be of Charles W. Crawford. He is wearing a patrol or "kepi" type cap, shirt, tie and jacket and appears to be a nice clean-cut young man. In his statement, designed to make him a sympathetic figure, he states, "I am sorry for my mother when she hears of this."

None of the newspapers, other than the local ones, ran the grizzly picture of Wilkin's body propped up and displayed in front of the bank. They did not have a method to transmit photographs any faster than the trains could deliver them.

Chapter Four: Adel's Most Exciting Day

THE BANK ROBBER

Adel did have telephone service in 1895, and A. F. Thompson of the telephone office was able to manipulate the telephone at a time when the excitement was at its highest and to summon parties from nearly every town in the county. Long distance communication was by telegram, however, and the telegraph office in Adel was a busy place. According to one newspaper, "Agent Fulmer had about 'steen newspaper correspondents to look after who were wanting to send dispatches in as many different directions." A telegraph operator from Des Moines was sent up Wednesday to help.

The telegraph office was at the railroad depot, two blocks from downtown. Many reporters were not happy because of that. *The Dallas County Record* reported "Wednesday was one of the days when there was good reason for registering a kick because the telegraph office wasn't at least within telephoning distance of the business part of the town. And a goodly number of them were registered, too."

None of the major newspapers ran corrections to the mistakes in their initial reports. Accuracy took a back seat to timeliness. Who would know, or care, what was correct and what was hype? For them, it was a one-day story.

The next day, March 7, Crawford was taken before Justice of the Peace Cole Noel, on a preliminary charge of assault with intent to commit murder, for the shooting of C. D. Bailey and S. M. Leach. Other charges would follow.

In Justice Court before Cole Noel J. P.
Preliminary Information
State of Iowa
vs.
C. W. Crawford

"The defendant, C. W. Crawford is accused of the crime of assault with intent to commit murder for that the defendant on the 6th day of March 1895, in the county of Dallas and State of Iowa with a shotgun .... and then loaded with gunpowder shot and bullets which said shotgun he the said C. W. Crawford in his hands there and then had and held in and upon on C. D. Bailey, then and there being unlawfully, willfully and with malice aforethought maliciously feloniously and with intent to kill and murder upon him the said C. D. Bailey did there and then make an assault, and the said C. W. Crawford in his hands

Chapter Four: Adel's Most Exciting Day

had and held then and there unlawfully, willfully, maliciously and with intent to kill, murder him the said C. D. Bailey did then and there shoot-off and discharge at and against the body of him the said C. D. Bailey, giving him the said C. D. Bailey aforesaid, there and then by the shooting aforesaid in the manner and by the means aforesaid, And so, the jurors aforesaid upon their oaths aforesaid do say that the said C. W. Crawford, him the said C. D. Bailey, in the county of Dallas aforesaid in the manner and by the means aforesaid unlawfully, willfully, maliciously, feloniously and with intent to murder him the said C. D. Bailey did make an assault, contrary to the terms of the statute in such case made and provided and against the peace and dignity of the state of Iowa.

J. D. Payne Sheriff Dallas Co. Ia.

That pretty well explains it, doesn't it? Without all the "legalspeak," and "aforesaids," I believe they are saying that Crawford shot Bailey. The charge in the shooting of S. M. Leach was just as wordy and confusing.

A warrant was issued for the arrest of C. W. Crawford, who was already sitting in jail, on a charge of assault with intent to commit murder. Sheriff Payne duly served the warrant and arrested Crawford. The next day, March 8, Crawford was again brought before Justice of the Peace Noel and bond was set at $5,000. Failing to give bond, he was returned to jail. It was now up to the grand jury to decide if these charges were warranted.

The indictment came on March 30, 1895.

"This indictment came into my hands for service on the 30th. Day of March 1895 and on the 2nd day of April 1895 I arrested the villain named C. W. Crawford and took him before the District court as commanded and now return this warrant served."

J. D. Payne Sheriff

Crawford did not have an attorney to represent him. He could not afford one and probably did not have any help from his family. He was a 19-year-old man in jail in a town whose citizens were more interested in lynching him than helping him. He was without education or skills. His intelligence is not known but considering the way he was so easily influenced by Wilkin he was probably considerably below the genius level. He was alone and on his own.

The Grand Jury hearing was held for Charles W. Crawford in Dallas County and was presided over by Judge Austin W. Wilkinson of Winterset. The following witnesses were interviewed, and their statements were presented: S. M. Leach, C. D. Bailey, Joseph Fair, J. D. Payne and T. J. Deaton. Their testimony mostly agreed on the main facts of the case. As to whether Wilkin or Crawford did the shooting, Bailey testified "I did not see the young man (Crawford) have a gun in his hands."

Leach described the scene when they first entered the bank and clearly put Wilkin standing behind Crawford. He then stated, "The man in the rear did the shooting." No witness ever placed a gun in the hands of Crawford.

Part one of the indictment was for the assault against S. M. Leach.

"With force and arms, in and upon one S.M. Leach, feloniously did make an assault, and the said S.M. Leach in bodily fear and danger of his life, then and there feloniously did put, and certain currency, bank bills, gold, silver and copper coin, the more particular description of which is to this grand jury unknown, amounting together to the sum of Two hundred,

Chapter Four: Adel's Most Exciting Day

seventy two and 30/100 Dollars of the value of Two hundred, seventy two and 30/100 Dollars of the money and property of the said S.M.Leach from the person and against the will of the said S.M.Leach then and there feloniously and by force and violence did rob,steal,take and carry away the said C.W.Crawford being then and there armed with a dangerous weapon,to wit: a shot gun, with intent, if resisted by the said S.M.Leach,him the said S.M.Leach then and there to kill or maim contrary to the form of the statute in such case made and provided and against the peace and dignity of the state of Iowa.

Count Two contained just as many "thens" and "therefores" as part one.

The said C.W.Crawford on the 6th day of March in the year of our lord one thousand eight hundred and ninety five in the county aforesaid, with force and arms in and upon one S.M.Leach feloniously did make an assault,and the said S.M.Leach in bodily fear and danger of his life did put,and sundry bank,bills,currency,gold,silver and copper coin,the more particular description of which is to this Grand Jury unnown,amounting together to the sum of Two hundred,seventy two and 30/100 Dollars of the moneys and property of the said S.M.Leach from the person and against the will of the said S.M.Leach then and there feloniously and by force and violence did rob,steal,take and carry away,the said C.W.Crawford being then and there and therein aided and abetted by a confederate whose name is to this Grand Jury unknown, the said confederate being present and armed with a dangerous weapon, to wit; a shot gun, with intent, if resisted by the said S. M. Leach, him the said S. M. Leach then and there to kill or maim contrary to the form of the statute in such case made and provided and against the peace and dignity of the state of Iowa."

(The mistakes in punctuation and capitals belong to the original transcriber and I have not corrected them in an effort to show, as accurately as possible, the way the document was presented.)

Crawford first pled "not guilty" to the charges. Then, on Saturday April 6, he appeared in court about 4 p.m., changed his plea to guilty and asked for immediate sentencing. Judge Wilkinson made a short talk to the prisoner and then gave the longest sentence he has ever given. "On the charge of robbery, a sentence of fifteen years as a general sentence, five years additional for shooting at S.M. Leach, the cashier of the bank, with the intention of committing murder, and two years additional for shooting at Postmaster S.M. Barr with the intention of murder. In addition to this sentence, which adds up to twenty-two years, he was indicted for shooting at C.D. Bailey, a prominent merchant of Adel, and upon his release from prison, he can be sentenced for this offense. Mr. Bailey is quite sick at present, as a result of the shooting, and for that reason, a sentence on this charge was withheld."

After his sentence, Crawford said he was expecting a longer term. He did not seem at all affected when the verdict was announced and seemed glad to be getting out of Adel, at last.

It would seem, by the charges, that Crawford held the gun and shot at Leach, Bailey and Barr. The indictment for "assault to commit murder," which is also on his official prison records, would also indicate this. Here is the code regarding attempted murder, in all its legalese:

707.11 Attempt to commit murder. 1. A person commits the offense of attempt to commit murder when, with the intent to cause the death of another person and not under circumstances which would justify the person's actions, the person does any act by which the

Chapter Four: Adel's Most Exciting Day

person expects to set in motion a force or chain of events which will cause or result in the death of the other person. 2. Attempt to commit murder is a class "B" felony. 3. It is not a defense to an indictment for attempt to commit murder that the acts proved could not have caused the death of any person, provided that the actor intended to cause the death of some person by so acting, and the actor's expectations were not unreasonable in the light of the facts known to the actor. 4. For purposes of determining whether the person should register as a sex offender pursuant to the provisions of chapter 692A, the fact finder shall make a determination as provided in section 692A.126. [C51, §2591, 2596; R60, §4214, 4219; C73, §3872, 3877; C97, §4768, 4773, 4797; S13, §4768; C24, 27, 31, 35, 39, §12915, 12918, 12962; C46, 50, 54, 58, 62, 66, 71, 73, 75, 77, §690.6, 690.9,

It is doubtful that the charge of assault with intent to commit murder would hold up in a modern-day court. Crawford, it seems reasonable to assume, never intended to commit murder. He probably never even intended to harm anyone. Nothing from the witnesses indicates that he ever had possession of the shotgun, much less *shoot off and discharge against the body of him the said C. D. Bailey.*

It would be difficult to determine, from the newspaper accounts alone, who actually did the shooting. The telegraph was the only fast method of long-distance communication that the reporters had at that time. But the cost of a telegram was billed by the word and the need for economy of words sometimes caused a distortion of the facts. It is amazing how inaccurate some of the accounts really were, especially on the matter of who carried what firearms and who shot whom.

Almost all accounts referred to the shotgun used as a Winchester although, in fact, it was a Spencer. Winchester was Spencer's biggest competitor and later bought the Spencer design when Spencer went into bankruptcy. This is an understandable error, however.

I have read versions of the story where the robbers carried out their crime using two revolvers (or six-guns), a revolver and a shotgun, two shotguns and even a rifle. It seems the only thing the newspapers didn't accuse the robbers of using was a cannon (or I might have missed that account). Both Wilkin and Crawford are credited with being the triggerman, and in one version they apparently pass the shotgun back and forth between them. The sworn testimony, however, tells a different story.

Judge Wilkinson certainly must have had more discretion in describing a criminal offense than is allowed today. He was able to charge Crawford with a crime that, from all appearances, Crawford did not physically commit. Crawford never held the gun and did not shoot Bailey or Leach, as he was charged. Had Crawford been able to hire an attorney and gone to jury trial, he probably would not have been found guilty of anything other than the robbery charge. The citizens demanded retribution, however, and it was given.

What pressure was put on Crawford to change his plea? Perhaps he saw the hopelessness of his situation on his own. Perhaps he was persuaded by the judge or sheriff. Perhaps he was scared for his life and just wanted to get out of Adel before the lynch mob returned.

In all probability, the robbery charge alone would have been enough to send Crawford to prison for 20 years, if the judge felt that was the term he should serve. On the bright side for poor Crawford, his social standing in prison was likely much higher as an attempted murderer than it would have been as a mere thief.

I am not a lawyer and have never been accused of being one. However, I am sure that people in the present time are much more informed about the law than were the citizens of 1895. After all, we grew up watching "Perry Mason" and "Matlock" on TV.

Within a half hour of the sentencing, Sheriff Payne, County Clerk of Court McCall and Crawford were on the train bound for Ft. Madison and the state penitentiary.

The Iowa State Prison, at Fort Madison, was already an old institution when Crawford became one of its guests. It was the oldest operating prison west of the Mississippi for many years. The prison was

Chapter Four: Adel's Most Exciting Day

established in 1839, one year after Iowa became a territory and seven years before it became a state. The Iowa State Penitentiary was patterned after the penitentiary in Auburn, New York and was a substantial facility. The historic old prison was replaced in 2015 by a new modern facility. Charles Crawford was assigned Iowa State Prison inmate number 6352, a number that would identify him for the next ten years.

County Attorney Edmund Nichols filed in September a motion to dismiss the charge of attempted murder against Crawford for shooting C. D. Bailey. He argued that the sentence already imposed was ample punishment and C. D. Bailey had fully recovered. Motion was granted in the January 1896 term of District Court. With both robbers dealt with, peace had returned to the town of Adel.

Why were the citizens so angry at the robbers that they shot one of them down in a volley of bullets, threatened to hang the other and then demanded a long prison sentence for him? Consider the times. Adel had been in existence only 50 years when the robbery occurred. The citizens had accomplished much in that short time span. They had built a town and a county. When Adel needed a railroad to preserve its county seat status, the town had leaders who knew how to accomplish it. When they needed a hotel, those same leaders stepped up and the citizens followed them. It was a community that worked together and took care of its needs. There was no government welfare system, but no one went hungry or without shelter. The citizens did not commute to another town for employment. They did not shop in another community. Most of them had no strong connections to any place other than Adel, and the community was like a big extended family. When their town was attacked by two robbers from outside the community, the citizens took it personally. It was their town that was invaded, their money that was stolen and their fellow citizens that were fired upon and left bleeding in the streets.

Convict Number 6352, Charles Crawford, was a model prisoner. His prison entry records show him as 19 years of age, single, Methodist and temperate (non-drinking). After ten years, the remainder of his sentence was suspended with two years of parole. He was given a new set of clothes and a train ride back to Adel. After quietly arriving in Adel, he found employment at the brick and tile works, for a time. But when his identity was learned, he found that even after ten years some anger still existed among the citizens. He soon left Adel and returned to Madison County. In Madison County, he began to put his life back together.

On February 10, 1909, he was married to Nellie Rogers in a ceremony in Winterset. His mother, L. L. Stith, signed as a witness. Charles and Nellie Crawford's only child, Lucinda, was born in 1915.

Charles Crawford was one of the first commercial truckers in Madison County, pioneering that field. After that, he was an employee of Madison County for many years, working with the roads department. He was also affiliated with the Odd Fellows Lodge in Winterset. There is no record of him ever breaking the law, other than minor offenses, after leaving prison. Charles W. Crawford died in 1953 at the age of 77. Many friends and relatives mourned his passing. He is buried in the Winterset City Cemetery. His nickname, Jess, is engraved on his headstone. He may have earned that nickname by likening himself to the famous bank robber, Jesse James.

Chapter Four: Adel's Most Exciting Day

Charles and Nellie Crawford

Over 30 years after the robbery, in a May 27, 1928 Des Moines Sunday Register newspaper article, F.M. Hoeye wrote to correct some erroneous information written earlier by a man named Frank Clarkson in a Los Angeles newspaper. He ends the article by stating that "A film company wrote a scenario of this robbery and offered Crawford a large sum to take the leading part, but he refused and begged them not to film it. This was during Governor Clark's last term and Crawford appealed to him to stop it and succeeded in doing so."

Sylvanis M. Leach recovered from his wounds and continued as cashier of the Adel State Bank. He was president of the bank when it moved into another new building on the southwest corner of the square. The Adel State Bank was merged with the First National Bank of Adel in 1927. The combined business continued until the bank holiday of March 1933. Senate File III, a depression era measure, allowed it to reopen and continue operating. However, it was forced to close for good in January 1935, a victim of the Great Depression.

Leach would not witness the failure of the bank to which he had devoted so much of his life and almost lost it for. He died in 1925 at the age of 75.

S. M. Leach's great grandson James Leach, served in the United States House of Representatives, as a Republican, for thirty years (1977-2007). He represented Iowa's second congressional district and chaired the House Committee on Banking and Financial Services. He is currently teaching as a visiting professor at the University of Iowa.

Cyrus D. Bailey was slower to recover from the effects of the buckshot. He did, in time, make a full recovery. His clothing store in Adel had been destroyed by fire just prior to the bank robbery. By 1896 he had a clothing store in Perry and had moved his family to that city. His successful business was an important part of the Perry business community for many years. He died in 1925.

George Washington Clarke continued his law practice and in 1900 he entered the world of politics. He served eight years as a member of the Iowa House of Representatives, the last four as Speaker of the House. From 1909 to 1913, he served as Lieutenant Governor of Iowa. In 1912, he was elected to the office of Governor of Iowa and was sworn in on January 16, 1913. In 1914, the popular Governor was elected to a second term. He retired from politics after his second term ended on January 11, 1917. He then served as Dean of Drake University Law School from 1917 to 1918. During Governor Clarke's tenure as governor, he worked to establish a state highway commission, endorsed restructuring and improving election procedures, advocated for workmen's compensation, and was involved in modifying and controlling investment companies. Former Governor George W. Clarke died on November 28, 1936.

Clark's grandson, Nile Kinnick Jr., stands with his grandfather among Adel's most honored citizens. Kinnick was born July 9, 1918 and grew up in Adel. He was an outstanding athlete, catching fastballs from Bob Feller (who grew up in nearby Van Meter) and leading the Adel football team to an undefeated season in 1933. He went on to the

Chapter Four: Adel's Most Exciting Day

University of Iowa where he led the legendary "Ironmen" football team and won the Heisman Trophy in 1939. He enlisted to serve his country in WW2 and lost his life on June 2, 1943 when his Grumman F4 fighter went down on a training exercise. Like his grandfather, Nile Kinnick Jr. was a true hero.

If this story has a hero, it would be Sheriff J. D. Payne. His actions, the day of the robbery, saved the life of a young man who, as it turned out, deserved another chance. Sheriff Payne followed the oath of office that he had sworn to and upheld the law in the face of an angry mob set on vengeance.

Unfortunately, a tragic accident cut short his life soon after he left office in 1900. He and his wife, along with some friends, had gone south to Louisiana for a winter vacation. The following tribute will supply the details of this tragedy.

Joe Payne, genial, kind-hearted and lovable, was accidentally killed by the cars, in February 1900, while on a pleasure trip south. The following sketch of his life and tribute to his memory was written by Clerk C.C. Pugh, who was intimately acquainted with the deceased.

Joseph Dunn Payne was born near Cambridge, Ill. May 20, 1856. He was the son of James and Elizabeth Payne. His parents brought him to Iowa during the first year of his life, but soon returned to Illinois, coming back to Iowa eight years afterward. Here Joe grew to manhood, attended school in Adel and taught in some of the neighboring districts.

In 1875 he was married to Miss Bell Crayne and to this union there was born one child, Ray, who is still living. February 22, 1887, he was married to Mrs. Emma Kimry, the lady who survives him and to whom this comes as a crushing burden. To this marriage a little daughter, Eva, was born, who lived but a few months.

On January 16, Mr. and Mrs. Payne departed for Louisiana with a party of friends southward bound. They intended to have a pleasant, joyous visit of two months when, after nearly six weeks of his visit had been spent, the accident occurred. It seems that he had gone to the post office and thence up the railroad track, used for switching, intently reading the paper. A train backing in rapidly was upon him before he realized its danger and in an instant, he was cruelly mangled beneath the death dealing wheels. The remains, accompanied by Mrs. Payne, Mrs. I.J. Mills and Dr. Ira D. Payne, were brought to Adel for interment. The funeral services were conducted by Rev. Gilbert Ellis of the Christian Church and the beautiful floral offerings testified to the esteem and love of the many friends of the deceased. The pall bearers were the county officers and ex officers, while honorary bearers were selected from the citizens of the town. The last sad rites were performed by the Odd Fellows and Knights of Pythias in the presence of a large crowd of sympathizing friends.

The account goes on to tell how well liked and respected J.D. Payne was. The tribute ends with the story of a little girl of the community who went to Des Moines on an excursion with the pupils of her school and was given money to buy her dinner. She went without dinner and took the money to buy flowers for Mr. Payne.

"Out of her heart came a welling of affection that she could go hungry and come home fatigued and worn bearing in her hands the roses that spoke more eloquently than words, how to her this deathbed brought a great sorrow. A nobler monument to Joseph Payne than might be erected out of marble more lasting than any imposing stone that might be reared over his grave, is the affection in the hearts

Chapter Four: Adel's Most Exciting Day

of the children that they have poured out on the altar of love and dedicated so sacredly to his memory".

The Payne family generously donated to the citizens of Adel, the shotgun used in the robbery and the teller cage from the Adel State Bank. These treasured items, from Adel's past, can be seen at the Adel Historical Museum.

The county coroner, H. A. Chappelear, held an inquest over the body of Orlando Poe Wilkin. Jurors were W. F. Brockway, Lea Thorton and Ed Taylor. The jury's verdict was that Orlando Wilkin had come to his death from gunshot wounds from the hands of unknown persons and without felonious intent.

In the far northwest corner of Adel's Oakdale Cemetery, three graves can be found almost out of sight of the rest of that beautiful and well-maintained burial ground. The place is referred to as "Potter's Corner." I suppose most cemeteries have such a place. It is a place where those who leave no one to mourn them, or to pay for their final resting spot, are buried. The three graves in this spot contain an immigrant woman from Serbia, another poor soul whose stone is no longer legible and a bank robber, Orlando Poe Wilkin.

Wilkin's body, after the angry citizens with their rocks and sticks and the coroner with his jury, finished with it, was placed in a rough pine coffin and unceremoniously buried in Potter's Corner. No one stood over the grave, as the coffin was lowered into the ground, and said kind words about the deceased. Perhaps there were no kind words to be said for such a man. There was no ceremony, no ritual, no sobbing and no singing. The city and county were obligated to bear the cost of burial and it would be done with a minimum of expenditure to the taxpayers.

The cemetery road that runs north along the old mill slough, that is now the main channel of the North Raccoon River, passes by many beautiful gravestones. It turns west as it reaches its northernmost point. To visit the lonely gravestone of Orland Wilkin, you must walk the short distance north from the road to the boundary fence line of Oakdale Cemetery.

It is difficult to imagine that in 1895, the cemetery would have ended at the point where the roads meet, and this road makes a turn to the north. From that point, it would have been timber and scrub brush, in 1895, with a narrow path back to the place designated as Potter's Corner. At that time, it was far removed from the rest of the cemetery. This shows how much disdain the citizens had for the robber that they buried his remains as far from the rest of the cemetery grounds, and the good people buried there, as was possible.

Most stories about the robbery, written or told after 1905, will include at the ending a brief retelling of a rumor that the body was dug up and removed from the grave by grave robbers. It is purported that the grave robbers were seeking a skeleton, or a body for medical science. This is difficult to disprove, or verify, as grave robbers seldom left accounts of their deeds and no one that I am aware of has exhumed the grave to check its contents.

It is well known that grave robbers practiced their trade in Iowa during this time. In 1893, a sting operation nabbed three of the worst of them in Des Moines. The Des Moines police were tipped off by a cab (horse and buggy type) driver that he had been hired to drive a party of men to Woodland Cemetery to rob a grave. The police captured three armed men as they were dragging the body of a recently buried Civil War veteran. The crime was traced to Drake University, which at that time operated a medical school in a building located at 5th and Mulberry Street, across from the Polk County courthouse. This medical school was discontinued in 1913.

The Iowa Medical Journal commented on the stolen-body cases in an attempt to justify it:

"Under existing circumstances and law, grave-robbing has become practically a necessity. The necessity demanding it is neither a mean or low one. The sole purpose for which graves are robbed is the acquisition of that knowledge of the structure of human body without which neither medicine nor surgery can be intelligently practiced,

Chapter Four: Adel's Most Exciting Day

and their inestimable results given to a suffering human race. Only by careful dissection of the dead can such knowledge be obtained. The motive, then, has in view the greatest good for the living generations on earth."

Regardless of these noble intentions, guards were placed around Woodland Cemetery, for a long time afterwards, to protect the deceased and their families from grave robbers.

Was Wilkin's body dug up by grave robbers? Here's an article from the Perry Daily Chief, dated March 29, 1905, that may shed some light on the subject. It is under the headline:

Orlando P. Wilkins...Finding Bandit's Remains Revives Bank Robbery...Interesting History of Famous Adel Robbery

The story, which is not attributed to any reporter, gives a fairly accurate account of the robbery. The last paragraph explains the headline and the reason for reviving the story ten years later.

"It was before the recovery of the injured businessman, several weeks preceding the conviction of the living criminal and a few days after the killing of Orlando P. Wilkins that his body was (words have been removed from the article but probably say "stolen from the") grave,"

The following is hard to read. My best guess is as follows: "destined to the so many (illegible word) in the old sacked corn lying vat, only to be uncovered after so many years in the old sack in a deserted barn in Adel."

Medical men needed human skeletons to study, in addition to cadavers, and the quickest way to obtain one was to submerge a cadaver in a vat of lye. The lye would strip all the soft tissue from the bones.

If there is any truth to this article, it leaves many questions unanswered. How was the body in the sack identified as Wilkin? The body would have deteriorated considerably in the ten years it lay in that barn. Was it identified by all the bullet wounds that would still be recognizable? Was the body reburied in its proper space or is his gravestone standing over an empty grave?

There is another possible explanation. The date of the article is March 29, 1905, ten years after the robbery and just three days before April Fool's Day, 1905.

The gravestone was not placed at the time of Wilkin's burial. It was sometime later that someone had the engraved stone set to mark his grave. Who it was is an interesting question. His family had moved to Montana and Wyoming and probably would not be visiting Oakdale Cemetery very often, if at all. Whoever had the stone placed there did not get the information correct, as the engraving on the stone gives the year of death as 1894, not 1895. It seems somebody was always getting information wrong when it came to Orlando Poe Wilkin.

We will never know why Wilkin chose the path he did. Born in 1863, he was a product of the aftermath of the Civil War, the same culture that created the "Wild West" with its lawless men and rough characters. Although he spent his youth in Madison County, a place better known for religious values and respect for society and its laws, his later environment must have had a greater impact on him. As a young man in the open ranges of Wyoming and Montana, he fell in with the wrong crowd. It was a time of conflict between the cattle ranchers, farmers and rustlers, a conflict that resulted in the Johnson County War of 1889 to 1893. Lawless men, such as Tom Horn and Nate Champion, set an example of ignoring the law and acting for their own benefit. Others followed this example and Orlando Poe Wilkin may very well have been one of them.

This does not excuse Wilkin's behavior. Other men lived with similar circumstances and did not turn to crime. His brothers, from what we have been able to learn, were law-abiding and respected ranchers in the unsettled ranges of Montana.

It is also very possible that Wilkin was suffering from some type of mental disorder. After the news of the robbery reached Minnesota, Warden Wolfer of Stillwater Prison made a statement to the newspapers concerning his former prisoner:

Chapter Four: Adel's Most Exciting Day

"O. P. Wilkin came to the prison from Clay County, January 27, 1891, to serve four years for grand larceny. He was released January 27 last at the expiration of his sentence. In April last, he had been paroled by the board of managers and while waiting to be sent out, made an attempt to escape by going through the gate. The parole was revoked at that time."

Warden Wolfer added that he thinks Wilkin was insane.

Was Wilkin insane? According to Warden Wolfer's statement, Wilkin was being paroled and while waiting at the gate to be released, he made an attempt to escape. That's insane enough for me!

If Warden Wolfer thought Wilkin was insane, as he stated in his dispatch, why would he allow him to go free? He probably had no choice but to release him from prison after completing his sentence, but couldn't he, or the state of Minnesota, have taken steps to put him in an asylum or, at least, a treatment facility of some sort?

There are many questions concerning the robber, Orland Poe Wilkin, that will probably be forever unanswered. The facts have been buried by the ensuing 120 years. Was he actually insane? Why did he return to Iowa after being released from prison, instead of Montana, where his mother and brothers resided? Why did he need money so badly that he was determined to rob a bank, in spite of the overwhelming odds against success? Who was the young lady from Wick who sent the letter he had in his possession the day he died? Is his body in the grave in Oakdale cemetery or was it removed by grave robbers? Who had the gravestone, with the incorrect year of death, erected over his grave?

After all these years, the answers to these questions can only come from our imaginations. Suppose the young lady from Wick had begun a romance with Wilkin by letter while he was in prison. They may have known each other as youngsters in and around Patterson. And suppose he returned to Iowa to continue the romance and wanted money to impress her. Suppose that after his death, in the bungled robbery, she is heartbroken but never reveals to anyone her feelings for a man of such questionable character. She saves her money and, years later, has a monument placed on the grave of the man who robbed a bank and lost his life for her. Well, it could have happened that way!

The following brief article appeared in the Winterset Madisonian newspaper regarding the two horses that pulled the buggy:

"W. W. Crawford got his horses and buggy, that Orlando Wilkin had borrowed, back from Adel. The buggy was considerably damaged, and one of the horses severely wounded by the pursuing posse, but it is thought, will recover. The other one was not hurt."

In a sad addition to another article, appearing in the Madisonian at a later date, we learn that the wounded horse was not so lucky:

"It is learned that the horse that was wounded by the shot from the pursuers, died Monday night."

In the end, good had triumphed over evil. That old adage, "crime doesn't pay," was, once again, proven correct. Vigilante law did not prevail, thanks to the courage of a dedicated sheriff and those brave men who came to his aid. One newspaper of that time even claimed that the vigilantes who participated in the Rainsbarger incident, several years earlier, were still active and present in Adel the day of the robbery. This claim has never been proven, however, but the langauge used in the article is interesting:

"In Dallas County, about half way between Adel and Des Moines, is the headquarters of the old vigilance committee which was engaged many years in following up the Rainsbarger gang and there are several members of the old committee living in the county who have been at the safe end of a rope with the noose at the other end."

The circumstances of that afternoon and evening, following the apprehension and jailing of the second robber, have been included in several subsequent studies of lynch mobs and their behavior.

Two people were given second chances that day. Charles W. Crawford was saved from lynching by a brave sheriff and his deputies.

Chapter Four: Adel's Most Exciting Day

Crawford used his second chance to become a productive citizen, family man and respected contributor to his community. In the end, he proved worthy of the second chance he was given. It was not wasted.

George W. Clarke went on to serve his fellow citizens as a leader of his community as a legislator, Lieutenant Governor and Governor of his state. After coming so close to losing his life at the hands of desperate shotgun wielding robbers, he certainly made the best of his spared life.

The robbery did not slow the march of progress in Adel. The same year as the robbery, 1895, saw the start of two major projects, the installation of a water system and the paving of the dirt streets.

As the twentieth century dawned, the automobile quickly replaced the horse and Adel, as well as the rest of the world, would see even more rapid change. The streets would no longer have hitching rails and the odor of horses would be replaced by the smell of gasoline fumes. Electric lights, telephones and indoor plumbing would soon make life better for all. There is much that the citizens of Adel have to be proud of. Its town center is graced by one of the most beautiful courthouses in the state. Its citizens had the sense to preserve Adel's historic brick streets and many of its scenic downtown buildings. Adel is, and always has been, one of the best places in the world to live and raise a family.

There have been many changes in the last 120 years of Adel's history, and there have been many exciting days. March 6, 1895, the date of the robbery of the Adel State Bank, will always be Adel's "Most Exciting Day."

Chapter Five

The Van Meter Visitor

As John Cleese, of the British comedy *Monty Python's Flying Circus,* would say, "And now for something completely different." I'm talking here of the "Van Meter Visitor." Unfortunately, there is no proof whatsoever that this creature ever existed outside of a spooky urban legend. All we have to go on are old stories, hearsay, and news reports from an era when exaggeration and fantastical stories took the place of television and video games. But it has become part of Dallas County's history and this book wouldn't be complete without a discussion of it. Maybe it doesn't fit into any crime category, there was no murder or robbery, but it certainly should be considered under the category of "mayhem."

The strange series of events began on the night of September 29 in the year 1903. An implement dealer by the name of U.G. Griffith was on his way home just after midnight. As he approached Van Meter, he is said to have noticed a strange point of light, like a spotlight, emanating from the top of a nearby building.

Griffith drove his buggy down the road to see what the source of the light was. As he approached it, the light moved all the way across the street to another rooftop, as if it had just simply flown through the air. It got even stranger when the light jumped away again off into the

Chapter Five: The Van Meter Visitor

night. Griffith was baffled as he sat there in the dark trying to make sense of what he had just seen.

Griffith was, by most accounts, an honest and well-respected member of the community. So, when he told others about the odd floating light he had seen the night before, they believed him.

The next evening, a piercingly bright beam of light, shining right in his face from beyond a nearby window, woke up Dr. Alcot, the local medicine man. He jumped out of bed, grabbed a gun and ran outside to see what was going on. What he saw startled the beejeebers out of the good doctor. There, right before his eyes, was a tall, human-like form with bat-like wings and a single horn on its head from which the blindingly bright light shot forth.

Dr. Alcot fired his gun at the strange beast, shooting it a total of five times. None of the shots seemed to have any effect on whatever it was. It didn't even flinch. The doctor decided maybe it was time to go back in his house and lock the doors. When he finally calmed himself enough to look out, the monster was gone. When Dr. Alcot reported his story, he was mostly believed. After all, doctors don't lie.

The town was excited. A creature with a piercingly bright horn, leaping from rooftop to rooftop, was beyond their comprehension. The situation would only be exacerbated by yet another sighting of something really weird the following day.

Clarence Dunn, the manager of the town bank, was worried that there were perhaps robbers to blame for the recent strange sightings. Brave as the first man who ate an oyster, he decided to keep a watchful eye on the little bank. When he arrived at the bank, around midnight of October 1st, he settled in with a shotgun he had brought along with him and waited for anything out of the ordinary to happen. He would not be disappointed. At approximately one a.m., Dunn heard a strange sound from outside, like someone gasping for air or being strangled. Sitting there in the dark, his sweaty fingers clinching the gun tightly as he watched every shadow, a beam of light suddenly penetrated the darkness. All that he could see was a shadowy figure lurking outside. Scared witless, Dunn fired his weapon at the beast, or whatever it was.

It then fled away into the night. Dunn had no doubt that his aim was true, and he had hit the intruder. However, the following day there was no trace of it and no blood. There was, however, some footprints. Not just ordinary footprints either. These footprints had only three toes. A plaster cast was made of the tracks, but it is not known just what happened to this cast.

The next evening, it was O.V. White's turn to encounter this strange visitor. White, a local hardware store owner, was roused from his sleep by a shrill, unearthly wail reminiscent of scraping or grinding metal. He quickly grabbed a rifle he had been keeping handy after hearing the reports of some strange creature roaming the night. When he peered through his window, he saw a strange dark figure perched up atop a telephone pole about 15 feet away. White took aim and fired at the creature. It was a direct hit, but this only caused the thing to snap its head up and stare at him as if irritated. White claimed he was then overwhelmed by a potent stench that hit him like a mule's kick. The stink was so strong and repugnant, it made him dizzy and caused him to lose consciousness. That thing must have had some really bad gas.

The Visitor…Probably a Doctored Photograph

Chapter Five: The Van Meter Visitor

Town of Van Meter Around 1903

Sidney Gregg, co-owner of the hardware store, was awakened by all of the ruckus and hurried to investigate. Once out on the street, he noticed a human-like winged monster descending from the telephone pole using its large, parrot-like "beak" to help. When it reached the ground, it stood up to reveal that it was around eight feet tall and had legs similar to those of a kangaroo. A light as powerful as "an electric headlight," leaped from its forehead. It took a look around and then darted off into the night in a series of leaps and bounds. After gaining momentum, it lit into the air on its giant wings.

It wasn't over yet. The following evening, October 3, J.L. Platt, Jr., manager of a tile and brick factory on the outskirts of town, heard a series of strange noises coming from the nearby abandoned coal mine. He described them as sounding like "Satan and a regiment of imps coming forth for a battle." When Platt went to investigate this eerie sound, he came face to face with the winged beast, looming at one of the entrances to the mine. This time there also appeared what seemed to be a smaller one of the creatures, both of which emitted a brilliant light from horns on their heads. The two creatures then took flight and were soon out of sight.

After this sighting at the old abandoned mines, many people came to the conclusion that the mines were perhaps the lair of the creature or creatures. After all, the mines extended underground into an extensive spiderweb of dark tunnels and caverns that would have been perfect for such beasts to take refuge within.

A posse of heavily armed men, carrying whatever weapons they could find, set up a camp at the mine's entrance. They were on the lookout for the creatures, should they return.

And they did indeed return the following evening, again at around one a.m. This was the moment. The group keeping vigil wasted no time in pouring lead from their guns at them. Strange as it seems, this had no effect at all. One newspaper report said:

The reception they received would have sunk the Spanish fleet, but aside from unearthly noise and peculiar odor they did not seem to mind it, but slowly descended the shaft of the old mine.

There was only one thing left to do. The mine was barricaded with rock and timbers and any other strong material they could find. It worked. The creatures were never seen again. Their legacy has lived on, however, with the tale being told and retold through the generations.

The story is chronicled in the book, *The Van Meter Visitor: A True and Mysterious Encounter with the Unknown*, written by Chad Lewis, Kevin Lee Nelson and Noah Voss.

The people of Van Meter have created an annual festival to celebrate this strange event. The festival is held in front of the Van Meter Library. Paranormal groups and vendors show up and create an opportunity for people to learn more about ghosts and the unknown. A walking tour, retracing the steps of The Visitor during those four days in 1903, is a feature of the event. People from all over the country come out to learn more about the winged creature. Whatever it was, ghost, alien or mystery animal, it continues to be a strange case that will probably never be adequately solved.

Chapter Five: The Van Meter Visitor

Artist's Drawing of the Visitor

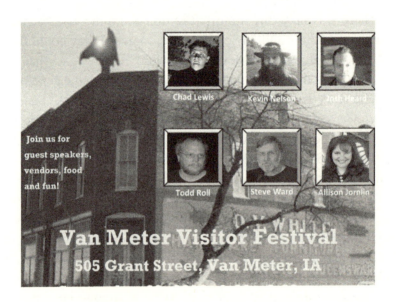

Chapter Six

Call Out the Dogs

Almost everyone in the county is familiar with The Hotel Pattee in Perry. But, have you ever wondered how it got its name? Me either, but there is an interesting story associated with Harry Pattee, the son of the man from whom the hotel took its name.

David Jackson (D.J.) Pattee, was a pioneer of Perry. Pattee was born December 22, 1839, in the county of Chittenden, state of Vermont. As a young man, he enlisted in the Ninth Vermont, and took part in the battles of that regiment, being captured at Harper's Ferry. While on parole, he was discharged for disability. He then came to Des Moines, where he again took a position as clerk. While here he, once again, entered the military service, this time in the Forty-seventh Iowa. Shortly after his re-enlistment, he was made lieutenant and later captain of his company. Upon his return from the army, he became a partner in the business where he had been clerking, and where his position had been kept open for him while he was serving his country. In 1867 he went to the new town of Perry, where he engaged in the mercantile business and afterwards the realty and loan business. In 1883, in company with another, he opened a private bank. Later the firm purchased the controlling interest in the First National Bank of Perry. After serving as Supervisor of the county for a year, mayor of the city three years and postmaster thirteen years, Captain Pattee was elected in 1883 and 1885 to the House of Representatives. He was Chairman of

Chapter Six: Call Out the Dogs

Hotel Pattee

some of Perry's municipal corporations and a member of several other important committees in the city. Mr. Pattee was an active member of the community. It is said of him, by those who ought to be familiar with his work, that no man has done more for the town where he lives than Captain Pattee. In 1903, he gave to the city a tract of twenty acres for a park. By then, he was one of the richest men in Dallas County.

Young Harry Pattee worked with his father in the bank and was very well liked. Harry's personal popularity was so great that it almost led to a lynching.

The story begins early in the morning of January 18, 1903, nine years before Harry Pattee and his brother William announced that they would build a three-story hotel on Willis Avenue to honor their father, David Jackson (DJ) Pattee. Harry Pattee and his sisters arrived at their home a little after one o'clock, after attending a dance. They entered the house quietly, so as not to disturb anyone, and went upstairs to their rooms. Harry had undressed and retired but he had only been in bed a few minutes when he heard a racket in the back yard. Thinking something was amiss, either at the barn or back porch, he went down the back stairway in his bedclothes to check it out. As soon as he opened the kitchen door onto the back porch, he saw a man. Unarmed and unprepared, Harry showed his pluck by grappling with the intruder. There was another man on the porch who, at the time Harry opened the door, was on a ladder.

Harry was struck a blow and fell to his knees. At that instance, the man he was grappling with pulled a revolver. Pointing it at Harry, he said, "Now I have you, G__ D__ you." With that said, he fired the gun. Only one shot was fired, after which the two intruders ran down the alley.

Although shocked and stunned, Harry was able to get up and stagger back into the kitchen. He went to the door to the back stairway and yelled, "Papa, come quick! I'm shot!" Mr. Pattee was sound asleep, after having made an exhausting drive to Bayard that day. He was quickly awakened by others, however, and bounded down the stairs.

Chapter Six: Call Out the Dogs

Finding Harry leaning against the doorframe, he assisted him to the sitting room and put him on the couch. The rest of the family joined them. Mr. Pattee phoned for Doctors Ross and Trout and notified central exchange of what had happened. Central assisted in calling George Grier, Marshall Reseter and Constable Dave Willis.

Dr. Ross arrived shortly after two o'clock and gave Harry a hypodermic to ease his pain. Dr. Trout arrived a few minutes later. They found the bullet had entered the right breast, just below the nipple. At first, the wound bled profusely but soon it was nicely dressed.

What were these men after? Turns out it wasn't money but pork, "the other white meat." Mr. Pattee had butchered two hogs and hung some of the meat on the porch roof. The men had taken a ladder and were helping themselves to the fresh meat hanging there when Harry discovered them. They had brought a gunny sack with them which was found at the scene. Everything was left just as it was, in hopes that daylight would aid in finding more clues.

A pack of hounds was called in and arrived by two o'clock the next afternoon. The hounds belonged to George Huffmier of Knoxville and C.H. Rinehart of Newton.

There was much interest in the hounds and the streets were literally jammed with people from the railroad depot to the Pattee home, a distance of three blocks. Patrolmen were stationed but they were unable to keep the crowds away. The militia finally had to be called out and they were successful in clearing the walks so the hounds would have a chance to work. The hounds were allowed to sniff around the porch for a time. Then, after going about the yard, they started west down the alley and then north. A block away, they lost the scent and came back. Getting the scent again, they hurried away to the north and east about three quarters of a mile. They went right through the city cemetery and stopped at the old post house located in a field on the north side of it. Stephen Crandell lived in this house, the very man they had suspicioned. He was immediately arrested. To verify the hound's accuracy, they were again put to work and followed the same trail the officers took in delivering Crandell to the city jail.

At a point some distance from the Pattee home, the hounds, when they first started out, ran in one direction for a way and then returned, striking away in a second direction. This second trail took them to the Crandell home. Later, they were put to work on this other trail which led to the McFarland house. McFarland and Crandell knew each other. McFarland, as it turned out, had been in jail with Crandell on a charge of stealing a hog from James Gravey. Crandell and McFarland had already been sentenced for stealing that hog and were out on parole. It was on the basis of that charge that Crandell was held at the city jail.

Three thousand people were out on the streets in the vicinity of the Pattee home. After the work of the hounds, excitement ran high, but the presence of the militia helped calm the crowds. The owners of the hounds credited the militia with keeping curious spectators from tarnishing the crime scene. They also gave credit to the people of Perry for actually wanting the perpetrators caught. "That is not always the case in many other crime scenes where we have worked the hounds," one of them stated.

Chapter Six: Call Out the Dogs

"I should think there were about five thousand people around the jail," Mr Huffmier observed as he left Perry. The situation was becoming quite serious. The militia had surrounded the jail all afternoon with fixed bayonets.

"Young Pattee seems to be a very popular young man and highly thought of," the other owner of the hounds, C.H. Rinehart added. "The boy insisted on seeing the dogs before we left, and I took them up to his room. He seemed to me to be resting easy and not suffering to any great extent."

After being threatened all day with hanging by an angry but disorganized crowd, Stephen Crandell was put safely aboard the seven o'clock train by Sheriff J.N. Haynes, City Marshall L.M. Reseter and three deputies. Sheriff Haynes rode the train as far as Dallas Center and then, leaving Crandell in the deputies' hands, returned to Perry to arrest McFarland.

Captain McKean of the Perry National Guard (Militia) sent a message to Iowa Governor Cummins informing him he had called out the company at the request of the Mayor and the Dallas County Sheriff. It was to prevent a lynching, McKean informed him. The law contemplates that only the governor can call out the guard, but Cummins had no criticism of McKean. He agreed that he would not have, in any way, interfered with the officer's disposition of his company under the circumstances.

Chapter Seven

Unsolved John Doe Murder of 1905

In 1868, there were only four towns in Dallas County, Xenia, Redfield, Wiscotta and Adel. Adel had a population of 600. All of Dallas County totaled around 8000. That year, 1868, was when the settlers of Dallas County, most of them along the rivers and streams, learned that a railroad was being surveyed between Des Moines and Fort Dodge. Since most of the land was open prairie, the railroad could be surveyed in a pretty much diagonal line, mostly in sight of the Raccoon River timberland. The Willis brothers owned land that the road would be crossing and so they set about creating a town. They gave 5 acres and 32 lots to the railroad with the understanding that the town would be named Perry, in honor of Col. Perry of Keokuk, an official of the railroad.

In 1881, the main line of the Chicago, Milwaukee & St. Paul came through Perry. At that time, the Milwaukee was the largest railroad system in the world. In 1882, Perry was successful in getting the Milwaukee line to locate its division station and shops on ground donated for that purpose northeast of town.

Perry was, for most of its early history, a railroad town, and its inhabitants were more transient than the citizens of the other towns in the county. Although, for the most part, Perry was a peaceful and

Chapter Seven: Unsolved John Doe Murder of 1905

pleasant town, this situation sometimes led to a higher incidence of mischief. The railroad could be blamed for bringing jobs, growth, prosperity and a few bad characters and lawless behavior to town. One such incident occurred in 1904.

The A.J. Caves family lived in a house on Lucinda Street in Perry. Their backyard sloped down to the Rock Island Railroad right-of-way near where the tracks crossed those of the Milwaukee Road.

It was in the middle of a hot Iowa August, after returning home from a ten-day absence, that the Cave family first noticed a very strong odor that seemed to permeate the area. Not thinking much about it, they went about their usual lives. On Saturday, August 20, while they were mowing a clump of tall grass that grew under a grove of Willows bordering the tracks, Mrs. Caves made a gruesome discovery. Hidden in the weeds and brush was the remains of a human body. She immediately notified Dallas County Coroner A.L. French.

Authorities began searching the area for clues. About 25 feet from where the body was discovered, they found a man's hat and $2.65, which would be about $85 at today's value. Drag marks led from that spot to where the body was found, indicating that the dead man was probably killed at that spot, and an attempt was made to hide the body. There was no sign of any kind of struggle, but considering how much time had passed, that was not unusual.

A coroner's jury was convened by French. The jurors were J.N. Partner, A.M. Harvey, and T.H. White. French informed the jurors that there were no distinguishing marks or scars on the man's body and nothing in his pockets to identify him.

The jury reported that: *The injuries were entirely about the head. The right side of the skull (was) crushed in, the temple and cheek bones (were) crushed and the right side of the skull (was) cracked. The blow which caused death was evidently delivered with crushing force.*

Hoping that someone could recognize him from their description, the jury also released the following information about the unidentified man: *Five foot eight inches tall, approximately 145 pounds, dark brown hair, teeth in good condition, wearing size seven shoes and in the lining of his hat was a clipping from the July 27 edition of the Des Moines News.*

The only other information the jury had was that some people had reported hearing what sounded like gunshots on the night of Tuesday, August 2. Even though they found no bullet wounds in the body, the jury used that date as the time of death. If that was correct, the body had been laying in the hot August heat for 18 days before being discovered. That would certainly account for the strong odor. In fact, the body was so decomposed that embalming could not be done to preserve it for identification.

The murder remains unsolved to this day and is listed in *Iowa Unsolved Murders Historic Cases*. It has been tagged *The Under the Willows Murder*. (Information was provided by Nancy Bowers.)

The murdered man was buried in an unmarked grave, his identity known only to God.

Chapter Seven: Unsolved John Doe Murder of 1905

UNEARTH GRIM TRAGEDY.

Decomposed Body of an Unknown Man is Discovered at Perry, Iowa.

Perry, Aug. 22.—With his skull crushed in, apparently by a terrible blow from some blunt instrument, the badly decomposed body of an unknown man was found lying near the Milwaukee tracks in this city Saturday evening. There were no marks for identification on the body, and thus far there is no clue to the name of the unfortunate.

From the Altoona Herald

Chapter Eight

Prohibition and the Roaring Twenties

By the turn of the 20th century, temperance societies were becoming prevalent in the United States and had found their way to Dallas County. The American Temperance Society, The Women's Christian Temperance Union and The Anti-Saloon League were all represented at one time or other. Together, they became a powerful political force in the county. Their parent groups were eventually successful in passing a national ban on alcoholic beverages. The National Prohibition Act, known informally as the Volstead Act, was enacted to carry out the intent of the 18th Amendment (ratified January 1919), which established prohibition in the United States. Here is a short history of temperance from *Hastie's History of Dallas County*:

The temperance question has always been a big problem, for liquor is almost as old as man himself. Among the early settlers of Dallas County, a few were given to drinking and subsequent ruin. Anderson Kelly was an early whiskey dealer. "An old man full of years and full of whiskey," was how one man described him. Kelly ran a whiskey shop in Penouch (later Adel). His source of supply was in Fort Des Moines. One winter, his supply ran out and he set out with a barrel

Chapter Eight: Prohibition and the Roaring Twenties

mounted on a tree forks sled drawn by a yoke of oxen to remedy this situation. He arrived at Jim Campbell's trading post in Fort Des Moines, secured his whiskey, and the next morning started for home. He had scarcely reached the open prairie west of the fort when a characteristic pioneer blizzard blew in from the northwest. The farther he went the worse the storm became. Progress became very slow and difficult. Finally, the weary oxen stopped, turned their backs to the wind and refused to proceed further. Kelly with a log chain hook, knocked the bung from the barrel and with a blue stem managed to suck his fill from the precious fluid. This gave him the encouragement he needed to continue on. Grabbing hold of the tail of the nearest ox, he compelled them to go with this ox goad, leaving the oxen to choose their own course. Finally, they reached the home of a settlor, where they remained overnight. Not until ten days later did the weather and trail conditions permit him to return for his barrel of whiskey. During this time, there was not a drop of whiskey at Penouch for his thirsty patrons. Upon reaching the barrel, he discovered that it had leaked fearfully during his absence from some cause and he was not slow in accusing old John Wright of being responsible for the leakage.

As far back as 1855 the people of Dallas County were pushing for the banning of spirits. In April of that year, they voted on a "Prohibitory Law." There were 233 votes in favor of the proposed law and 164 opposed.

The whiskey crowd was not satisfied, however. Two years later, Benjamin Bennett and 180 others petitioned the District Court to submit a vote to the people on a license plan. The plan would have allowed limited sales of alcohol under regulation and license. Accordingly, on the first Monday in April 1857, an election was held. The results were against the license plan by a good majority, and the temperance principles of the county were maintained.

The temperance cause grew steadily. The W.C.T.U., Good Templar Lodges and other temperance clubs were formed in many of the county's communities. But despite the noble efforts of good people, bootleggers and unscrupulous merchants would not hesitate to violate the law, "for some men would sell the shirt off their own back to secure the accursed thing." Others would stoop to anything for money.

In most of our history, the people of Dallas County, and of the state of Iowa, have not favored the liquor traffic, but it has been an almost constant source of trouble and agitation. *Our better state officials have well expressed themselves when they caused to be inscribed on the walls of the state capital these words, "Nothing is politically right that is morally wrong."* (Hastie)

Never in our country's history has a law failed so completely as prohibition. From the very beginning, it was ignored by citizens and those who were supposed to enforce it. Passage of the Volstead Act was the beginning of a period known as "The Roaring Twenties," a period that ended with the stock-market crash of 1929. Here are a few incidents from that period.

April 1, 1921…Sheriff Gets Another Still

Pete Stefani was a coal miner who lived near Dallas Mines. He got himself in bad with the law when he decided to engage in the business of manufacturing liquor.

Sheriff J.W. Stacey visited the Stefani home and found the still in his basement, along with one hundred gallons of mash and liquor. "He was fixed to turn out a lot of raisin whiskey, but now he has nothing to show for it except his court summons," the sheriff commented.

Not only did Pete face a fine, or jail sentence, but his plant was wrecked and the materials for booze making confiscated.

Chapter Eight: Prohibition and the Roaring Twenties

April 9, 1924...Des Moines Booze Car Sold at Adel

Judge W.S. Cooper ordered two slot machines confiscated by the sheriff be destroyed. One machine was taken from The Jacob Pool Hall in Adel and the other was taken from the oil station at Gardener.

Judge Cooper also issued an order authorizing the sheriff to sell, at public auction, a Ford car taken from Ernest Couch, 1304 Main Street, Des Moines, Iowa. Couch was arrested for transporting liquor. Seven gallons of whiskey was found in the car when he was picked up.

January 14, 1925...Des Moines Legger is Jailed at Adel

The above headline is from the Des Moines Tribune. "Legger" was a shortened version of bootlegger. I found many instances where bootlegger was shortened to "legger" by the newsmen. Bootlegging was so prevalent during this period that it led to the creation of a new term.

Verne Hooker of Des Moines was arrested Monday night at Bouton by Sheriff S.J. Nuzum and Deputy Lew Stanley. At the time of his arrest, he had in his possession, in a Ford coupe, twenty-five gallons of alcohol.

He was brought to Adel and arraigned in court. He pleaded guilty to a charge of bootlegging and Judge W.S. Cooper sentenced him to spend one year in the Dallas County jail.

Hooker indicated that he could pay a fine, but the judge said he believed a jail sentence would do more good.

April 9, 1926…Farmer was able to find some prohibited liquor

Even though drinking alcohol was against the law, it was still available and those caught abusing the rules of drinking and driving were always able to come up with excuses.

Fred Woodyard, an Adel farmer, was found guilty in district court, by Judge J.H. Applegate, of driving while intoxicated.

Woodyard blamed a bump on the head for his actions following a collision between his car and another at the time of the alleged offense.

Oct. 28, 1926…Robert Adams Arrests Nine on Liquor Charges

Robert Adams was a well-known G-Man in central Iowa. His official title was Federal Prohibition Agent but the "Leggers" usually preferred G (for Government) Man.

G-Men worked with local officials to enforce the prohibition laws. Sometimes these local officials invited them and sometimes the G-Men invited themselves. This time, Adams invited himself but received the cooperation of Dallas County Sheriff Sam Nuzum.

Adams and Nuzum, along with two Dallas County deputies, were quite successful in their raid into Dallas County. They arrested a total of nine men for liquor violations.

Four arrests were made in Gibbsville. A quantity of wine and beer was seized. The unfortunate bootleggers were Carl Jones, Cisto Ferri, Joe Nizzi and Tony Caponi. Yes, Carl Jones does seem a bit out of place in this group. Now, you're probably asking just where in the heck is Gibbsville. Well, I'll save you the trouble of Googling it. Gibbsville is almost straight north of Granger about 2 ½ miles and just a short jaunt west of highway 17 on the south side of the Des Moines River. It's north and west of The Saylorville Reservoir.

The posse next moved on to Moran in their pursuit of the demon spirits. There they arrested Isabella Dezorzi after discovering 190 gallons of wine and a quantity of moonshine in her home.

Isabella wasn't the only scofflaw in the little town of Moran. Sisto Cananrari had the cuffs slapped on his wrists for the third time in two years. Sisto was in possession of two hundred bottles of beer and 170 gallons of wine. State officers, Adams proclaimed, will attempt to make Sisto a resident of the state penitentiary as a repeat offender. Moran is probably better known than Gibbsville, but just in case you haven't spent much time touring the northeast corner of Dallas County and Des Moines Township, Moran is straight west of Gibbsville on highway 141. The town was once a railroad station and was named after William Moran, a nearby farmer.

The last stop for the raiders was Zook Spur. Since I've filled you in on Gibbsville and Moran, I'll do the same with Zook Spur, although probably not necessary. Most good citizens of Dallas County already know where Zook Spur is. This former coal mining town is just west of highway 17 and about three miles south of Madrid. It's on the Dallas/Boone County line. Zook Spur was at the end of a railroad spur line which ran from the mail line to a coal mine operated by the Scandia Coal Company under the management of a man named H. Zook. In this tiny town they arrested the last three of their day's catch. Jim Stewart, C.C. Gilliland and Bob Parks were all nabbed at the Gilliland home. The spoils here was a large quantity of beer, "Made by authority of prescription," according to Adams. No information is available on who the doctor was that wrote the prescription.

Murder and Mayhem in Dallas County

May 25, 1929...Robert Knote Arrested in Booneville on Rum Charge

Who was Robert Knote and what is a rum charge? Let's tackle the first question first. Knote first gained notoriety by getting blasted out of bed at a Des Moines home. "A bootlegger's war was blamed by police for an explosion of a bomb at the home of Thomas F. Conroy, one of eight men convicted in federal court here in the Peoria-Des Moines liquor conspiracy case, which was on appeal to federal court. Conroy and his wife were not home but Ray Haubert and Robert Knote, both said by police to have been involved in the liquor traffic here, were thrown from their beds uninjured. Some damage was done to the house. The place was fired on recently, presumably by members of a liquor faction."

April 4th of that same year, 1927, we find Mr. Knote mentioned in an article under the headline "Begin Liquor Drive" A general drive was opened on liquor law violators Saturday by Carl Missildine, County Attorney, who filed injunction and liquor nuisance actions against a score of defendants. The list included Dominic Passio, Robert Knote, Clarence Sunderleiter, Robert Hocking, Roy Harnett, Claude Brown and etc.

The famous Robert Knote honored our jail with his presence a couple years later on May 25, 1929. "Robert Knote Arrested in Boonville on Rum Charges. Robert Knote, listed on police records as from Des Moines, is in the Dallas County jail in Adel. He will be given a hearing on a charge of driving a car while intoxicated. Knote appeared in Boonville community Thursday afternoon driving a rented car. He drove the

Chapter Eight: Prohibition and the Roaring Twenties

machine into the yard of the Elmer Paulin home, made a race track out of the premises and attempted to force an entrance into the house, police said. Mrs. Paulin phoned to Boonville for assistance and a crowd of vigilantes went to the farm and overpowered Knote, who gave up after a hard fight. Deputy sheriffs from Adel arrived soon afterward and Knote was brought to jail here."

Knote went on to become one of Des Moines' more conspicuous hoodlums. After many more charges involving liquor, both selling and consuming, he gained his greatest notoriety in 1945 during what was known as the "Polk County War." A civic committee asked Governor Robert Blue to remove County Attorney Francis Kuble and Sheriff Vane Overturff from office after a raid on Knote's nightclub, "The Mainliner". Knote was charged with conspiracy in violation of both liquor and gambling laws.

Just imagine, Knote was once a guest in our humble little jail on a "rum" charge.

Dallas County had its share of bootlegging, rum-running, moonshining and all the other crimes associated with prohibition. But, during this period it also had several crimes not associated with alcohol. Let's take a look at a few of those.

White Robes and Hoods in Perry

A large gathering was held on the grounds of Washington Township School in the summer of 1923. Many citizens responded to the appeal of the group sponsoring the gathering. Soon, this group had a large membership in Perry, with many coming from nearby towns. What was this group? It was The Ku Klux Klan.

Murder and Mayhem in Dallas County

In 1923, a wave of unusual activity was sweeping the country and the Ku Klux Klan, a secret organization, was at its height. Thousands of people were joining this society across the nation. Some of the Klan's strong beliefs were restricting foreign immigration, advocating for tough law enforcement, loyalty and patriotism and discrimination against Catholics, Jews and Negros.

We have all seen pictures of the Klan's white robes and hoods. And, we are all familiar with the Klan's strict secrecy and burning of fiery crosses at their meetings. But who would suspect such a thing to take place in Dallas County? It did, and more than once. A big mass meeting in celebration was held at the fairgrounds in Perry on the evening of September 24th. One of the largest crowds ever assembled in Perry came from far and near. Many were just curious to see and hear more about this strange group. What they saw and heard was an excellent display of fireworks, followed by the burning of an immense wooden cross.

A similar meeting was held at the fairgrounds again the following May. During the warmer months, they often held their private meetings in the open fields of their rural members.

6,000 people packed into the Perry Fairgrounds on Sept. 24, 1923 for a Klan meeting. About 2,000 Klansmen and Klanswomen were present for the semi-public meeting. The celebration started with a parade around the half-mile track. After the parade, the Rev. J. H. Williamson gave an address entitled, "The Making of America."

Iowa's largest Klan ceremony was held in Perry at the fairgrounds in June 1924. 15,000 attended, including more than 5000 Klan members. The address of the day was entitled, "Making America Great Again."

One of the largest funerals ever held in Perry was for Walter Schell, a prominent farmer and Klansman who died at King's Daughters Hospital. On a cold Jan. 22, 1925, more than 200 Klansmen

Chapter Eight: Prohibition and the Roaring Twenties

and some 1,500 people from Perry attended services at the Christian Church and then formed a huge cross over his grave.

As you might guess, some of the Klan's policies were not too popular. The divisions it fostered between Catholics and Protestants was seldom to the advantage of either. And the agitation at election times was as bad as any of the election mischief of today.

This was a time when the country was engaged in the failed experiment of prohibition. The criminal justice system had expanded to meet the challenges prohibition created. Police arrested many more people and a disproportionate number were immigrants, black, poor and working class. Many people read the daily newspaper stories of raids and bootleggers and concluded the law wasn't doing enough to stop them. That's a big reason why the Klan became so powerful in the twenties.

But after the stock market crash of 1929, the country was plunged into a deep recession. The Klan's program for making America great again was suddenly not working. Members started dropping out like rats leaving a sinking garbage barge, and in a few years the Klan in Perry was mostly just a bad memory.

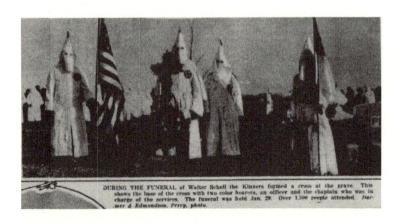

Funeral of Walter Schell in Perry

July 21, 1923...Murder of Homer Davidson

It all started over $2. Homer Davidson made the fatal mistake of selling his fellow farmhand, Harold Gillispie, a tent on the installment plan for a total of $4. The installment plan, apparently, was half now and half when you can catch me. Gillispie had paid the first installment of $2 in Perry that day and when he went to the farm of Blaine Smithson, their employer, to get the tent, Davidson refused to turn over the property until the second $2 installment was paid. Gillispie claims that he finally told Davidson just to keep the tent. After he had started off in his car, Gillispie said that Davidson called him back to the barnyard. He picked up a wrench, put it in his pocket and went to meet Davidson. He then hit Davidson over the head and left immediately in his car. "It was self-defense," he claimed.

Harold Gillispie was a drifter, or floater, who was described as "hard-boiled, not likable but always able to get work because he was an exceptional farmhand." Originally from Kirksville, Missouri, Gillispie, 25, was a big man, six feet tall and 150 pounds.

Witnesses to the fight claim that Gillispie first struck Davidson with a wrench, knocking him to the ground. The next blow he struck was the fatal one. Gillispie brought his knife straight down on Davidson's skull, breaking through the bone and penetrating the brain.

The fight took place at the Blaine Smithson farm southwest of Perry. A farmer in a nearby field saw them clash and came to Davidson's assistance. He called a doctor and, together with other neighbors, cared for the man and took him to the hospital. Davidson was taken to King's Daughter Hospital in Perry where doctors gave him almost no chance to live.

Gillispie left in a roadster with one of the witnesses, an 18-year-old fellow farmhand named Charles Sloan. Sheriff J.W. Stacey and two deputies rushed to the scene to investigate. They immediately started a

Chapter Eight: Prohibition and the Roaring Twenties

manhunt for the two and enlisted the aid of several police departments and the state.

Very early the next morning, five a.m. to be precise, Gillispie and Sloan were arrested in Yale, Iowa. They were said to be on their way to South Dakota and had parked their car in front of a garage in Yale. When they returned to the car, the sheriff was waiting for them. Gillispie was made a guest of the county at its jail facility in Adel. He was charged with assault with intent to commit murder. Sloan was also provided a room in the county's graybar hotel but was later released. Sheriff Stacey stated that "Gillispie will be held on the charge pending the condition of his victim. If Davidson dies, as expected, he will probably be charged with murder."

Davidson was reported at the time (11 o'clock that night) as resting with a chance of recovery. It was also reported that he had been knifed three times in the fight. True to the doctor's expectations, however, Davidson passed on to eternity without ever giving his side of the story.

Trial was held in Adel on September 24, 1923. The jury consisted of six men and six women with Judge W.S. Cooper of Winterset presiding. County Attorney Harry Wifvat was the prosecutor and Charles Howard, one of Des Moines' negro attorneys, appeared for the defense. The state, in its opening statement, asked for the death penalty.

Charles Sloane was the first witness to testify for the state. He stated he had witnessed the encounter between the two men and Gillispie had struck Davidson with a wrench, knocking him down. He then struck a second blow. Mrs. Davidson, wife of the slain man, was the second witness. Her testimony corroborated the testimony of Sloan.

The trial lasted just two days. On September 26 at 5 o'clock in the evening, after approximately six hours of deliberation, the jury returned a verdict of manslaughter.

Immediately after hearing the verdict, Gillispie waived the formality of setting a date for his sentence. Gillispie would not be needing that tent unless the roof at the Men's Reformatory at Anamosa sprung a leak. He was immediately sentenced to spend the next eight years there as a guest of the good people of Iowa.

February 16, 1921 – Sheriff Unknowingly Raided Crap Game.

It was a Sunday afternoon. Dallas County Sheriff John Stacey and his friend, Clarence Powers, decided to go into the wilderness and do a little target practice. They carried with them an armload of artillery and a pocket full of ammunition. The guns were 44's of which it was said at the time they "speak a wicked langauge."

The two crossed the bridge east of Adel and cut down through the brush where their bullets couldn't hurt anyone. As soon as they started shooting, several men started scurrying over the hills and valleys like a flock of scared rabbits.

It was soon discovered that the sheriff had unwittingly raided a crap game. Several well-known citizens were seen headed in the general direction of Van Meter with their hands in the air and their feet scarcely touching the ground.

January 31, 1924…No Clews in Adel Oil Station Holdup

(Yes, it is actually spelled "clews" by the Des Moines Evening Tribune reporter)

Officers have gained no clew to the two men who brutally beat up Lloyd Conant, manager of the Standard Oil Station in Adel, which they robbed of $8 yesterday noon.

Chapter Eight: Prohibition and the Roaring Twenties

Conant broke the arm of one of the men with a wrench before they got the drop on him and it was in revenge that they slugged him. Conant is a World War (1) veteran.

July 25, 1925…Wins Wife in Foot Race at Adel

It must have come as a shock to Mark L. Jenkins when he was arrested in Los Angeles, California on a charge of bigamy. It was only eight months earlier that he had taken the hand in marriage of a Mrs. Salome Helen Kramer in Hollywood, California. The officials who arrested Mr. Jenkins claimed that he was already married, and this marriage was bigamous.

We don't know all the details of this story, but we do know this much from the newspaper reports: Mark Jenkins was an automobile salesman living in Adel in 1919. He also had lived in Des Moines and possibly a few other locales. He somehow became involved in a foot race for which the prize was the hand of a girl. Jenkins had no desire to marry the girl, he claimed, but nonetheless he put on his early version of Nikes and won the race in spectacular fashion. Just who his rival was for this dubious prize was not revealed.

Jenkins celebrated his victory by participating in a spectacular wedding ceremony, which he believed to be a staged wedding as part of an advertising scheme. Imagine his surprise when he later discovered a bona-fide license had been issued and he was legally married to the damsel. He stated he only knew her as Miss Wuerst and did not mention a first name. That must have been a little awkward during the wedding ceremony.

Jenkins also told the officers that after learning of the marriage license, he informed the manager of the race that he must obtain an annulment. Perhaps he was a little too trusting as he said he left immediately after that, believing that his request would be carried out.

The unsuspecting bachelor married his present wife on December 24, 1924. All was not bliss in this marriage, however. This Mrs. Jenkins claimed that he also had married a woman named Mrs. Elma Rogers, who lived at 750 Seventy-eight Street in Des Moines. There was no Seventy-eighth Street in Des Moines at the time and the city directory did not list a Mrs. Elma Rogers.

Now, I'm sure you have as many questions as I do. Unfortunately, this is all the information I was able to uncover on this stirring and heart wrenching tale.

November 18, 1927...A Nervous Chicken Thief

A thief backed his truck up to the henhouse on the John Nixon farm near Adel and loaded into it 100 of Mrs. Nixon's best young chickens. Officers were notified and, two nights later, the chickens were returned, the thief evidently fearing to dispose of them. The thief may not be a chicken, but he had his henhouse ways.

Chicken thieves and chicken thefts were a plague during the depression and hard times when 26 of every 100 people had no work and there were no minimum wages. The Great Depression was a chicken era. There were chickens on every farm, Leghorns and Plymouth Rocks and Rhode Island Reds. Gathering eggs was a daily chore for most farm kids. Chickens were valuable, not only for their eggs but for meat. Women became experts at preparing chicken because they did it so often. There was no Colonel Sanders or KFC in that time. After all, who would buy prepared chicken from a man dressed as a southern gentleman and claiming to have a secret recipe?

Chapter Eight: Prohibition and the Roaring Twenties

February 3, 1928…Farm Employee Fined for Beating Mules

Stealing chickens and making bootleg hootch weren't the only crimes in Dallas County during the Roaring Twenties. Consider this crime that occurred near Dallas Center. Cecil Coffman, a farm hand employed by Roy Eikenberry of near Dallas Center served a ten-day sentence in the county jail in lieu of a $35 fine imposed upon him by Justice of the Peace Hoover of Dallas Center for beating a team of mules. He entered a plea of guilty after information was filed against him by humane society officers. Coffman used an end gate rod in an effort to make the mules pull harder.

September 11, 1929...Heavy Smoker Robs Adel Drug Store

The headline read "Robbers Victimize Adel Drug Store"...Robbery of the R.E. Morril drug store at Adel, Ia. Monday night was reported Wednesday to Des Moines detectives by W.F. Glen, Adel deputy sheriff. Loot from the drug store, according to Detective Glen, included a gun, 4,000 cigarettes, two Kodaks, two wrist watches, another watch and two clocks.

July 1, 1930...More Chicken Thieves

By 1930, Dallas County, as well as the rest of the country, was beginning to feel the effects of the stock market crash and the general bad economic conditions. As a result of the growing unemployment, men began figuring out new ways to put bread on the table, not all of them legal. There was one chicken stealing gang in Minnesota, three young men, who got 45 chickens from a farm one night and 60 the next night. Five different farms in one week. Their downfall was their car. It had two Riverside tires on the rear wheels and a Pathfinder tire on the front. The County Sheriff tracked the thieves from their "car prints."

Here's a story about some men in Dallas County who took chicken-thieving to new highs:

Two men who detectives claim have admitted they have "made their living stealing chickens since last fall," were in city jail in Des Moines and two others, said to be their companions, were in jail at Adel where they were arrested Saturday night.

The two Des Moines men were J. M. Hunt, Seventh and Porter streets, and Weslery Letze, 518 East Fifth street. They are being held for Adel authorities.

Chapter Eight: Prohibition and the Roaring Twenties

Detectives claim the two men at Des Moines and one of those at Adel have admitted theft of more than 700 chickens within a radius of 200 miles of Des Moines. Detectives also recovered a shotgun, silverware, a talking machine and a clock, which they claim the men stole from a house near Perry.

The two men at Adel were captured by authorities after a chase of several miles during which, the authorities claim, the men threw several sacks of chickens out of their car. Now that's something you don't see every day.

Chapter Nine

Boonville Bandits

It was a spectacular daylight bank robbery that ended in a spectacular failure. Three bandits attempted to rob the little bank at Boonville but hadn't counted on someone being prepared for just such an event.

The fun started shortly after 9:30 a.m. on February 10, 1925, when the leader of the bandits, a young hooligan named Harold Leighton, walked into the bank carrying weapons with intent to clean out the vault. The assistant cashier, W. J. McCallister, was the only one in the bank. "I was at home at the time, Cashier C.C. Cook explained. "Our home is just next door to the bank. Suddenly Mrs. cook happened to look over at the bank. She saw McAllister through the window. He had his hands up. Someone is robbing the bank, she told me. I got the shotgun immediately. It was loaded. I started for the bank." Leighton had two accomplices for this adventure. Neither proved to be a very good choice for this type of work, however. Alfred "Ace" Oliver was a Negro (I'm not being politically incorrect, that was the term used back then), who claimed to be a jazz orchestra leader. Sylvester Lampman was a Des Moines taxi driver.

"The Negro, Oliver, was standing out in front acting as watchman," Cook said. "He didn't see me for a few seconds. When he did, he started to run. I would have taken a shot at him but a woman on her way to the post office got into the line of fire. I didn't dare shoot.

Just then, Leighton came out of the bank. He had a gun in one hand and carried a bag of money in the other. Under his arm he held his hat, which was filled with money. Both of us fired about the same moment. His bullet missed me. I fired again. He stumbled on a few feet."

Several shots were exchanged but Leighton's bullets all missed Cook. Leighton fell in a pool of blood after he had gone about 20 feet. Cook turned in the alarm at once.

Leighton was found to be carrying three guns, two 44-caliber and one 32-caliber. All of the money, $3000, was recovered.

"I heard McAllister," Cook continued. "He was shut in the vault trying to make me hear. The bandit had made him go in there. The vault wasn't locked. I got McAllister out. In a few minutes a posse formed and went after Oliver. Before that, the other fellow, Lampman, who was with the car up on the hill, drove down to the bank. He must have started when he heard the shooting. He surrendered at once. He had no gun."

Lampman, the third member of these three stooges, had been stationed several blocks away with his car. When he heard the shots, he drove up to the bank and immediately surrendered. He was unarmed and driving his Des Moines taxi. No mention was made whether he left the meter running through this whole caper.

A posse was quickly formed, headed by Compton of the Van Meter State Bank. They got Oliver about a mile and a half from town. He had thrown away his gun and offered no resistance. Sheriff Nuzum took Oliver and Lampman to Adel where they were housed in the county's jail.

An ambulance was called from Des Moines for Leighton, who had buckshot wounds in his upper arm, his chest, his throat and one in both thighs. He was given an inoculation against lockjaw by physicians at Boonville before the trip. The ambulance, with driver William Strait and detective Sherman Delmege, had fought through a 25 mile stretch of nearly impassable roads in their efforts to reach the wounded man. The trip, because of the condition of the roads, took nearly three hours, and on one occasion the front axle was repaired by a mechanic in order to continue the trip. The heavy ambulance slipped into the ditch several times on its way to Boonville. Such was the condition of Iowa roads in 1925.

The return trip, with Leighton aboard, was made without mishap. Apparently determined to show a stoic resistance to pain, Leighton lay quietly on the ambulance stretcher on the trip from Boonville to Des Moines. His eyes were closed. His face was touched with blood from the wound on his jaw. Although he answered no questions put to him, he turned restlessly once and called for "Marie." He was evidently in considerable pain, as he winced when he made several quick movements on the stretcher. Although quiet on the trip, Leighton was nearly hysterical from pain and loss of blood when he arrived at City Hospital.

City Hospital, as you may have figured out, is now known as Broadlawns Medical Center. Since this book is about history, it is altogether proper that we explore the history of this hospital. In 1903, Drake University built a medical school at 406 Center Street in Des Moines. The building was utilized for nine years, and then it stood empty until 1915. Two physicians and a private investor purchased the building and established a miners' hospital. After extensive remodeling, the facility was incorporated under the laws of Iowa in 1916 as the Miners' and Industrial Workers' Hospital. A total of 35 beds were available for either miners or charity patients of Polk County. Two years later, the Presbyterian Synod of Iowa purchased the facility and renamed it the Presbyterian Samaritan Hospital. Because the Synod was unable to redeem the property's bonds, the facility was

Chapter Nine: Boonville Bandits

returned to the previous owners. A friendly lawsuit was filed in order to clear the title and property, and the hospital was eventually sold to the City of Des Moines for $95,000. During World War I, under city management, the hospital was developed as a venereal disease institution. It was known for a period of time as the Indigent Hospital but, in 1919, the name was changed to the Des Moines City Hospital. The Des Moines Health Center was also housed within the basement of the hospital. In 1913, the Iowa Legislature had authorized Polk County, among other counties, to care for tuberculosis patients who resided within the county and at the time were being cared for in tents at the County Farm. A 60-acre tract of land was purchased at 18th and Hickman Road for $64,000, and construction began in late 1922. The new building opened in April 1924. The first buildings erected consisted of a 60-bed tuberculosis unit and a 30-bed nurse dormitory. As a result of a naming contest, the name Des Moines City Hospital became Broadlawns. A nurse from the Iowa State Tuberculosis Association suggested the name for the hospital because of the spacious lawns where the hospital was located. Now you know.

By noon the following day, it was reported that there was little change in Leighton's condition, according to physicians. "The wound in his jaw and throat makes eating almost impossible and talking extremely difficult," they informed the reporters.

Officers were able to extract some information from Leighton, however. He confessed to heading the gang that had staged nine successful robberies in and about Des Moines. Leighton confessed that he and his gang had staged robberies at DeSoto, Earlham, Van Meter, Dexter and Waukee and that the previous Monday night the trio had driven to Johnston station to rob the oil station there. He also confessed, the Sheriff said, to robbing the Wood store and the Monteith store (Guthrie County). He blamed Oliver with having caused the attempted robbery at Boonville to fail.

Mrs. Marie Stevens, Leighton's alleged sweetheart, was taken into custody by Sheriff Findley that night. Mrs. Stevens was living in a rooming house at 711 park St. She was questioned by the Sheriff, who attempted to learn if she was implicated in the earlier robberies. She was not.

C.C. Cook, in one of many interviews after the robbery, said the following: "Was I excited? No, I really can't say that I was. You see, I had been preparing for just such a circumstance for 15 years. I kept a loaded shotgun in my home. I kept it there for this very purpose. I figured that some time I would need it. That time was yesterday. I'm sorry I had to shoot Leighton but, you see, it was a business proposition, really. Not much different from endorsing a check or making out a deposit slip. I hope Leighton recovers."

Leighton did recover, but the bullet in his throat remained forever. "The bullet that crashed into his jaw was embedded in his throat, and he will probably carry it through life," a staff physician at the City Hospital, where the bandit was a patient under guard, stated. "The swelling in the throat, due to the wound, makes a diet of liquid nourishment necessary."

No one was permitted to visit the prisoner patient. If he had any relatives, none had attempted to communicate with him. Leighton claimed Philadelphia as his home so, perhaps that wasn't surprising.

On March third of that same year, Harold Leighton was given a life sentence after he pleaded guilty in District Court. He collapsed after the sentence but was quickly revived and taken straight to Fort Madison Prison. He had been in the hospital at Des Moines and Perry since he was wounded at the bank and was probably still in a weakened condition.

Chapter Nine: Boonville Bandits

L. to R. "Ace Oliver, Sylvester Lampman, Sheriff Nuzum

Twenty days later, on March 23rd, Judge Applegate sentenced "Ace" Oliver to spend the next 35 years in the Anamosa Reformatory. He was represented by George F Brooks of Des Moines. Brooks told the court that Oliver was about 21 years old and had served a year in Indiana for larceny. Here's how the newspaper reported it: Adel, Iowa March 21st. Alfred Oliver, Negro, was sentenced to 35 years in Anamosa Reformatory by judge Applegate this morning. He was one of the three Boonville bandits who held up the bank there a month ago. I guess, back then, before political correctness, it was important to emphasize Oliver's race. Judge Applegate said that he would not consent to recommend a parole before the minimum term had been served.

The last of the three bandits, Sylvester Lampman the taxi driver, was still in jail and had not plead guilty as the other two had. I was unable to verify his sentence, but I suspect it was in line with the other two.

Chapter Ten

Murder of Fred Wernli...Stay Away from My Daughter

On a quiet Sunday morning the streets of Woodward suddenly became the scene of a bloody shooting. It was springtime, May 24, 1931, and the weather was warm in the little community in the north part of the county near the Dallas/Boone county line. People were leaving churches and heading home to prepare a Sunday dinner for family or head out to a favorite spot to do some fishing. They had just endured a long cold winter and, now that it was fit, they were anxious to be outdoors. The country was in the midst of a great depression, but the people of Woodward were still able to find ways to enjoy life in this friendly family-oriented community. It was not a scene where you would expect a cold-blooded murder to occur.

The trouble had begun the previous summer when Ray Taylor, 40, tried to bring charges against Fred B. Wernli in Boone County for molesting his ten-year-old daughter. The grand jury dismissed all charges against Wernli and completely exonerated him.

Taylor again tried to bring charges against Wernli in the following March term of the Boone County District Court, but that attempt also failed.

Chapter Ten: Murder of Fred Wernli

Fred B. Wernli was considered a wealthy farmer. The 56-year-old man had been married only three months but had a family from a previous marriage. Ralph, the only son, lived with his father while his daughter Violet taught school at Glenwood and his other daughter, Mrs. Glen Rhoads of Sioux City, was a housewife.

Ray Taylor had come to Woodward shortly after World War One. He had been living part of the time in Woodward and part of the time on the farm of his father-in-law, Henry Kruse, three miles from Woodward in Boone County. The Kruse farm was where Taylor's children lived. Kruse had rented his 80-acre farm to Fred Wernli but the lease had expired that winter. Taylor's father-in-law, Henry Kruse, had placed Taylor under a restraining order to keep him away from Kruse's farm which was near Wernli's 120-acre tract. Kruse had also asked Dave Skiles, Woodward mayor, to be appointed his guardian.

Wernli had come to town that Sunday to meet Mrs. J.P. Carroll with whom he intended to ride to Des Moines to visit his wife. Mrs. Wernli had gone to Des Moines the day before to visit friends.

On that fateful Sunday morning, Wernli was stopped on Main Street by Taylor and, after exchanging a few words, Wernli crossed the street and joined a group of men in front of Charles Myer's Billiard Hall. "I hope he comes over here and repeats in front of you men what he just said to me," Wernli told the men as he stepped up to join them. Taylor came toward the group and inquired of Wernli what he had just said. Receiving no answer, he repeated the inquiry and again failing to receive a reply, drew a revolver and fired a shot which struck Wernli. Wernli fell to the ground.

When Wernli raised to face his accuser, after he had been mortally wounded by that first shot, he said "You've killed me. I never harmed anyone."

Taylor replied, "Well you _____, that's what I wanted to do. You attacked my daughter."

To this Wernli replied, "I never did it." Taylor fired four more shots and, after stepping back a few feet, pointed the gun at Wernli again and snapped the trigger twice more. Four bullets entered Wernli's body, three in the abdomen and one in the right arm, fracturing it.

Harvey Faulkner, who was spending his Sunday morning in a pool hall instead of church, heard the shots and came running outside. He grabbed Taylor and held him until constables Ray Vernon and Lyon Stuber could come and arrest him.

The four men on the bench that morning were C.B. Pierce, J.T. Carrel, Frank Guthrie and his son, James Guthrie. James Guthrie's guardian angel must have been on duty that Sunday morning as a stray bullet pierced his shoe but left no injury.

Wernli was unconscious after reaching Iowa Methodist Hospital. An operation was performed to stop the flow of blood, but to no avail. Death came at 5 p.m., eight hours after the shooting.

Taylor was taken to the Dallas County jail in Adel where he was questioned by Sheriff Clint Knee. Knee quoted Taylor as saying, "I had to do it." But Taylor refused to answer any other questions until he was represented by an attorney.

A coroner's jury was held the following Monday night in the office of Woodward Mayor D.J. Skiles. The jury was composed of C.F. Cosby, D.G. Skiles and William M. Wade, justice of peace. They heard evidence of the Sunday morning killing for more than three hours.

Chapter Ten: Murder of Fred Wernli

Ray Taylor

Fred Wernli

Chapter Ten: Murder of Fred Wernli

George Sackett, Dallas County attorney, who assisted corner L.H. DeFord of Redfield in questioning witnesses, announced upon receipt of the verdict that he would file charges of first-degree murder against Taylor.

While authorities were taking the first step in investigating the killing, Taylor was pacing the floor of his cell in the Dallas County jail at Adel and relatives of the slain man were making final plans for the burial of the victim.

Attorney Sackett endeavored to obtain a signed statement from Taylor before coming to Woodward for the coroner's inquest but reported that Taylor refused to discuss the shooting or prior events. 13 witnesses appeared before the jury, including James Guthrie, a Woodward dog breeder whose shoe had stopped one of the bullets fired by Taylor. A large crowd gathered to hear the testimony but was denied admittance to the mayor's office. Witnesses were brought in one at a time and the only outsiders present were newspaper men and three relatives of Wernli, his son Ralph, A.G. Rhodes, son-in-law, and H.L. Savage a brother in law.

The jury gave little credence to the unsubstantiated accusations against Wernli involving molestation of Taylor's daughters. Justice of Peace Wade declared that Taylor had held ill will against Wernli for more than a year and that the Boone County Grand Jury had investigated charges made by Taylor and found them to be groundless.

Wernli had an excellent reputation. All witnesses agreed on that. Several witnesses, including Ray Vernon, constable, testified that Taylor's reputation was questionable. Kenneth Dixon, local barber, testified that Taylor came to his shop about two months prior and waited until he was alone. Taylor then approached him with a proposition to buy a revolver which Dixon had for sale. "After he inquired about the price, I told him I guessed I would keep the gun as I was planning a trip this summer and might need it," Dixon testified.

When questioned by attorney Sackett as to his reasons for not making the sale, Dixon replied, "I didn't figure his reputation rated my selling him the gun."

The gun, empty shells, the bullet which caused the fatal wound, and a comb case and pair of glasses and case taken from Wernli's clothing were exhibits at the inquest. One of the bullets had struck the glasses and comb case in the inside pocket of Wernli's coat and lodged there. The case bore evidence of the shooting.

Other inquest witnesses were C.B. Pierce, Harvey Faulkner, Frank Guthrie, Dan Newell, Charles Myers, H.L. Savage and Pat Chase. Chase, a deputy Sheriff, testified regarding the gun and Taylor's admittance to jail.

The jury found that the killing of Fred B. Wernli, was unjustified and that Taylor acted with "felonious intent" and "without provocation." They recommended that Taylor should be held on murder charges for action of the grand jury at Adel.

Trial was held in district court in Adel the following September. After hearing the case, the jury deliberated 25 ½ hours, before Judge W.S. Cooper of Winterset called them back in to ask if they had reached a verdict. When the foreman answered that they had not, the judge gave the jury further instructions and sent them back for more deliberation. After another one and a half hours, the jury was able to return a verdict of guilty of first-degree murder with a recommendation of life in prison. On October 19, 1931, Taylor was sentenced to just that, life imprisonment in Fort Madison penitentiary, by judge W.S. Cooper of Winterset.

Attorneys for Taylor filed motion for a new trial. The motion was overruled by judge Cooper. Attorneys based their grounds for a new trial on charges that one of the jurors, Alta Russell, had talked about the case to Charles Potter and Emerson Maxwell. Potter and Maxwell were placed on the stand and they both denied that Miss

Chapter Ten: Murder of Fred Wernli

Russell had told them anything about the case. Defense attorneys said they would appeal the sentence to the Iowa Supreme Court. Sheriff C.A. Knee escorted Taylor to Fort Madison that same Monday afternoon.

On January 21, 1932, The Iowa Supreme Court handed down their decision. Taylor was denied his appeal.

Chapter Eleven

Virgil Untied...Minburn Shootout

Lena Hagenstein looked up from the magazine she was reading and glanced at the clock on the wall above the switchboard. Yawning, she noted it was still a couple hours before dawn. It was ghostly quiet at this time of morning, and even though she was used to working the overnight hours at the Minburn Telephone Exchange, this night seemed to go especially slow. In spite of the boredom, Lena felt fortunate, in those days of The Great Depression, to even have a job.

The little town of Minburn is in the northern part of Dallas County along highway 169. It was once a busy railroad town, shipping livestock and grain on the M. and St. L. Railroad. It has never had a population much over 400 and today it is the home to 379 people. It is also one of the friendliest towns in Iowa, and maybe the world. It is not the place you would expect a gun battle resulting in murder to take place. But that is exactly what happened on the night of Thursday, July 23, 1931.

Minburn had its own telephone exchange, as many small towns did in the days prior to "Ma Bell." In those days before automation, an operator was required to be on duty at all hours of the day and night. If a farmer's prize cow was having trouble calving in the middle of the

Chapter Eleven: Virgil Untied...Minburn Shootout

night, he expected to be able to reach the veterinarian by phone and that required an operator.

Lena Hagenstein had been tending the telephone exchange, or plug board, that night. The Minburn Exchange plug board consisted of one row of ¼-inch bantam jacks fronted by several rows of phone cords, each of which was connected to a phone subscriber line. When a caller picked up the receiver, a light near the plug would light and Lena would switch into the circuit and politely ask, "number please?" If the request was for a local number, Lena would push the plug into a local jack and start the ringing cycle. If, on the other hand, a number outside of the exchange was requested, she would plug into a hand-off circuit to start what might be a long-distance call. The call would then be handled by subsequent operators in another bank of boards or in another building miles away.

Lena usually didn't handle many calls after mid-night, especially on a Thursday night. It was the early morning hours, before dawn, which were the slowest and most boring. That was about to change, at least for this night.

As Lena sat there in the quiet, she suddenly heard noises coming from the Gottschalk Grocery Store next door. She had no way of knowing that safecrackers were at work, but she did know something was wrong. She quietly picked up the main line from her operator's phone and pushed it into the connection for Virgil Untied's phone.

Virgil Paul Untied, part-time night watchman for Minburn, was born on February 14, 1898 in Frazeysburg, Muskingum County, Ohio. His parents were Charles Owen Untied and Mary Jane Mortimor Untied. He married Elsie C. Sundby on October 24, 1917, and had three daughters, Mildred age 12, Doris Virginia age 10, and Afton age 7.

Virgil quickly woke from his sleep and answered the call. He assured Lena he would be right there and asked Lena to connect him to Lena's brother, William Hagenstein. After explaining to William what was happening, he asked him to meet him downtown. Virgil next asked Lena to connect him to his younger brother, Jasper Untied, and asked

Jasper to meet him downtown. Jasper was also a part-time night marshal for the town of Minburn.

By the time the three men arrived, the robbers were at the E.J. Shaw Grocery store. This store was near the railroad depot. It was later determined that it was the fourth store in the little town that they had robbed that night.

After determining the location of the robbers, the two deputies hid themselves at the depot with guns drawn. Virgil bravely crossed the railroad tracks and approached the Shaw Grocery demanding surrender. That's when gunfire erupted in the quiet little town and the night turned deadly. A dozen shots were fired from the building. Virgil Untied lay dying.

The three suspects made a quick dash to a car that they had parked a block away. It was reported it had Polk County (Des Moines) plates on it. They made their getaway, heading south on highway 169 towards Des Moines.

Law enforcement agencies in Dallas County, Polk County and Des Moines were quickly notified. An attempt was made to stop a speeding car that matched the description of the getaway car, between Grimes and Johnston. Another gun battle ensued and the suspects, once again, eluded capture. A Special Agent, Sam Nuzum, was appointed by the BCI (Bureau of Criminal Investigation) to assist local law enforcement authorities in solving the crime. Nuzum was familiar with Minburn, having served as Dallas County Sheriff from 1924 to 1930.

Virgil Untied was taken to King's Daughter Hospital in Perry, suffering from a shotgun slug that passed through his right eye and lodged in the brain. He also had two shots in the abdomen, one in his right leg and one in his left shoulder. Four days later, on July 27, Virgil Untied passed away, his wife and three children by his side

Chapter Eleven: Virgil Untied...Minburn Shootout

Virgil Untied

Murder and Mayhem in Dallas County

August 3, eleven days after the shootout, Des Moines police captured three men after a gunfight that wounded one of them. The men were attempting to burglarize a pool hall in Des Moines. These men, Ronald Hast, 21, Ralph Smith, 22, and Tom Egan, 30, were suspected of being involved in safecracking and other illegal activities in the area. Neither Jasper Untied or William Hagenstein could positively identify them. Unfortunately, they could not be tied to the murder of Virgil Untied and the case remains unsolved to this day.

These events took place in the summer of 1931, a very different time from today. The average annual wage, for those fortunate enough to have a job, was $1850. Gas was 10 cents a gallon. The world was waking up to the fact that the crash of 1929, and the resulting depression, were not going to be short-lived. To make matters worse, the Midwest was suffering a crop-killing drought. It was the year that Al Capone began a 17-year prison sentence in Alcatraz for tax fraud. It

Chapter Eleven: Virgil Untied...Minburn Shootout

was also the year that a Texas girl, Bonnie Parker, met a small-time hoodlum named Clyde Barrow. It was a difficult, trying and lawless time. And it would get worse.

Virgil Untied is honored on the Officers Down Memorial Page and The Iowa Department of Public Safety Peace Officer Memorial Page. His story is also included in the Iowa Unsolved Murders Historic Cases under the title *Gun Battle in the Night*.

What was gained by this senseless murder? Four businesses in the little town were robbed of the following: tires and innertubes from Minburn Oil Co., $5 from the Butler Garage, $20 from the Gottschalk Grocery and between $100 and $200 from the E. J. Shaw Grocery. For that a good man lost his life!!

Chapter Twelve

Attacked with an Axe

It was December 5, 1932, a Saturday evening. The scene was near Perry along the Raccoon River. When officers arrived at the cabin (or shack) owned by Charles Pickett, they found a grizzly sight. Roy Haywarth's body was lying on the ground in a nearby plowed field. He had suffered a shotgun blast to the head and arm from a double-barreled 12-gauge shotgun. It could have been worse. Only one barrel of the gun functioned, but he was shot twice with that one barrel. The officers included Perry Police Chief Tim Graney, Albert Nicholson, Grant Herrold…a Milwaukee Railroad detective, and John McCarthy.

The altercation apparently started earlier that evening when Haywarth rapped on Pickett's door. Pickett, who was snot-slinging drunk, claimed that Haywarth had attacked him with an axe. Pickett then shot him with a 12-gauge double-barreled shotgun.

Two neighbors of Pickett, Ed Reed and Chauncey Cole, had driven into the drive by their cabin, after returning from a nearby farm, and saw Pickett with a wheelbarrow. He was about 100 feet from their home in some plowed ground. When Reed and Cole went in their cabin, Pickett followed them in. He was obviously drunk and remained only a short time. Reed followed him as he left and found him with Haywarth's body on the wheelbarrow. Pickett was attempting to move the body to the river, but in his inebriated state he had fallen to the

Chapter Twelve: Attacked with an Axe

ground and wasn't having much success. He offered Reed ten dollars to dispose of the body. Reed refused. Reed returned to his cabin and he and Cole drove to Perry to report the slaying.

After discovering the body, the officers surrounded Pickett's shack and officer Herrold went to the door. He rapped loudly and ordered Pickett to come out. Pickett unlocked the door and allowed the officers in. He then attempted to resist and was quickly handcuffed.

The floor, immediately inside the door of the Pickett cabin, was blood stained. The shotgun used in the killing was leaning against the bed near the south wall of the front room. It was still loaded. In the back room of Pickett's cabin, officers discovered five barrels of rye mash. That would help explain the intoxicated state that Pickett was in.

Prohibition was the law of the land in 1932. It would end the next year, 1933, with the passage of the 21st amendment. The Volstead Act had been in effect for 12 years, by 1932, and had pretty much lost any respect it might have had. Violations were becoming quite commonplace.

Outside the cabin, the wheelbarrow was back at the front door and Haywarth's body had not been moved from where Reed first saw it. Haywarth was fully clothed, except for one shoe which had probably been pulled off when Pickett put the body in the wheelbarrow.

Pickett was arrested and taken to Perry where he was locked in jail. The next day, he was driven to Adel and arraigned for the murder of Roy Haywarth. Pickett admitted to Sheriff Clint Knee that he had shot Haywarth after he had rapped on his door. He claimed that Haywarth had attacked him with an axe before Pickett shot at him with the 12-gauge shotgun. He also told Sheriff Knee that Haywarth was in the habit of taking his meals at the Pickett cabin. An examination of Haywarth's stomach revealed no food and no alcohol. Haywarth, 42, was a WW1 veteran.

In attempting to reconstruct the crime, officers concluded that one shot was fired at Haywarth while he was back of the stove in the southeast corner of the rear room. The other shot was fired as he was near the front door, as evidenced by the bloodstains.

Pickett was tried in Adel on a charge of murder of Roy Haywarth. The state asked for the death penalty, claiming that the murder was premeditated and Haywarth was shot in the back. The defense claimed it was self-defense. The case was given to a jury of six men and six women at 11 a.m. Friday January 27, 1933 and they deliberated until midnight. Resuming Saturday morning, they brought the verdict in at 10 a.m.... guilty of manslaughter. Judge W.S. Cooper of Winterset had given the jury five possible verdicts: First degree murder with death by hanging, first degree murder with life imprisonment, second degree murder, manslaughter or acquittal.

Pickett was sentenced to eight years at Fort Madison Penitentiary.

Charles Picket

Chapter Thirteen: Bonnie and Clyde at Dexter

IOWA MACHINE GUNS ROUT BARROW GANG

Linked by Radio, Planes and Autos Pursue Fleeing Leader After Two Are Seized.

SOUGHT IN FOUR MURDERS

Discovery of 'Wild West' Camp Brings on Battle in Which Three Outlaws Are Badly Wounded.

DEXTER, Iowa, July 24 (AP).— Clyde Barrow, notorious Texas outlaw, fought a machine-gun battle

Chapter Thirteen

Bonnie and Clyde at Dexter

Streams of sunlight were just starting to pierce through the trees on that July morning in 1933. Bill Arthur looked at his watch and noted it was just past 5 a.m. It was almost deadly silent. The only sounds were the chirping of crickets and a few birds off in the distance. He and C.C. "Rags" Riley had been waiting, hidden in the brush, since just after mid-night and his neck and shoulders were starting to ache. Dallas County Sheriff Clint Knee, Dexter Town Marshall John Love and two other men were hidden nearby. They were part of a posse of over 50 lawmen and volunteers that had started assembling at the old abandoned park the night before.

There were five of them at the campsite they had been watching, three men and two women. The campers had started a fire and two of the men were busy preparing breakfast. There were two cars parked beside the campsite, a 1932 Ford V8 and a Buick. The Buick was riddled with bullet holes.

In an instant the silence was broken. One of the men in the opening heard something and instantly yelled out, "Get the hell out of here you Sons-a-Bitches or we'll kill you!" That was how it began.

Bonnie Parker and Clyde Barrow are perhaps the best remembered outlaws of the era, at least in Dallas County. There is good reason for that as they had a great impact on our history. Bonnie and

Chapter Thirteen: Bonnie and Clyde at Dexter

Clyde traveled with their gang throughout the Midwest, robbing banks, stores, and gas stations. Newspapers followed their exploits, making them famous throughout America. They had established quite a reputation in the Midwest as thieves and murderers and had killed several police officers. These fugitives from the law were always on the move, trying to keep one step ahead of the "laws," as they called them.

The town of Dexter, in the southwest corner of Dallas County, was an unlikely place for a shootout. Founded in 1868, the town was named after a popular racehorse. The town was also known as the place of manufacture of hand-cranked washing machine and a type of hog oiler called the "Dexter Hog Oiler."

Dexter, in 1933, was on a very busy road and had more than 70 businesses along its main street, including a dozen gas stations. The people of Dexter were used to having lots of strangers in town, although they found it curious that one certain car was always backed into its parking space and left running. Everyone knew each other in the friendly little town. That's why, when these strangers arrived that hot July, the townsfolk were suspicious and even fearful of them. Clyde made several trips into Dexter to buy food and medical supplies. Not knowing who Clyde Barrow was, the townspeople sold them the things they needed. During the Depression, if someone came in with cash money to spend a merchant was going to do business with that person and not ask many questions. The local police officer, John Love, who also worked in a clothing store, sold him shoes, shirts and socks.

The gang had chosen the remote location of the old Dexfield Amusement Park and set up their camp on a wooded hilltop overlooking the park site.

Dexfield Park had opened in 1915 and was, at one time, one of the most famous amusement parks in Iowa. It was located between Dexter and Redfield on the south side of the Raccoon River. Every Sunday, people would come from miles around, including Des Moines, and often there would be over 4,000 people there. In addition to a large cement swimming pool, fed by the nearby Marshall springs, there was a long line of drinking fountains on the south side of the pool. The spring water was said to have healing qualities for arthritis sufferers. Dances were held in the large open-air dance hall on Sundays, and sometimes during the week. On the south side of the pool was a large pavilion with a cement pool and restaurants on both the east and west ends where pop, ice cream and sandwiches were sold. The park also featured a movie screen, a Ferris wheel, a shooting gallery and stands, a skating rink and skate rental, a bridge and bayou with canoe rental, a baseball field and a free camping ground. The now abandoned park had been closed a few years before the Bonnie and Clyde gang arrived.

Along with Bonnie and Clyde were the other gang members, Buck Barrow, Buck's wife Blanche, and a teenager named W.D. Jones. Buck, Clyde's older brother, had been severely wounded just days before in Missouri.

The gang was on the run from that big shoot-out with police in Platte City, Missouri, a small-town north of Kansas City. They had been in the Dexter area four or five days, intending to hide out, rest and recuperate. In addition to Buck's gunshot wound, Blanche had glass shards in her left eye, and Bonnie had third-degree burns from her ankle to her hip, a result of Clyde's not seeing a Road Closed sign and running off a bridge and flipping into a ravine. Sources disagree on whether there was a gasoline fire or if Parker was doused with acid from the car's battery under the floorboards, but she sustained third-degree burns to her right leg so severe that the muscles contracted and caused the leg to "draw up." Jones observed that "She'd been burned so bad none of us thought she was gonna live. The hide on her right leg was gone, from her hip down to her ankle. I could see the bone at places." Parker could hardly walk; she either hopped on her good leg or was carried by Barrow.

The three had rendezvoused earlier with Buck and Blanche, and hid in a tourist court near Fort Smith, Arkansas to wait for Bonnie's burns to heal. After Buck and Jones bungled a robbery and then

Chapter Thirteen: Bonnie and Clyde at Dexter

murdered Town Marshal Henry D. Humphrey in Alma, Arkansas the five-member gang had to flee, despite Bonnie's grave condition.

Next, the gang checked in to the Red Crown Tourist Court south of Platte City, Missouri. It consisted of two brick cabins joined by garages. The gang rented both. To the south stood the Red Crown Tavern, a popular restaurant among Missouri Highway Patrolmen. Owner Neil Houser, who had become suspicious, told William Baxter of the Highway Patrol, a patron of his restaurant, about the group.

Clyde and Jones went into town to purchase bandages, crackers, cheese, and atropine sulfate to treat Bonnie's leg. The druggist had been asked to watch for strangers seeking such supplies and he immediately contacted Sheriff Holt Coffey. Coffey, who had already been alerted by Oklahoma, Texas, and Arkansas law enforcement, put the cabins under surveillance. The sheriff also contacted Captain Baxter of the Highway Patrol. Baxter called for reinforcements from Kansas City, Missouri, including an armored car. Sheriff Coffey led a group of officers toward the cabins at 11p.m, armed with Thompson submachine guns.

The .45 caliber Thompsons were no match for Clyde's .30 caliber Browning Automatic Rifles (BAR), stolen on July 7 from the National Guard armory at Enid, Oklahoma. When a stray bullet caused the horn on the armored car to blast continually, the police officers mistook it for a cease-fire signal and let the gang make their get-away. They seemed to have had enough after that and did not pursue the Barrow vehicle.

The Barrow Gang had arrived in Dexter with one car. Due to Buck's condition, they needed a second one and decided to go "car shopping" in Perry. They selected (stole) a 1933 Ford belonging to Ed Stoner. Clyde was a great fan of Fords. In fact, he wrote a letter to Henry Ford telling him how much he liked his cars. Ford used Clyde's letter to sell more cars.

Buck Barrow was in bad condition. The bullet that struck him was later described by Dr. Chapler as a "through and through" head wound in the front part of the skull where no vital organs are contained.

The wound was unbandaged and Buck's brains were exposed at the time he was captured. They had cleaned the wound several times by pouring hydrogen peroxide into it and letting it boil all the way through. The only other treatment available was aspirin, which Buck said helped with the headache pain (Excedrin headache number 33?). Right after he was shot and before she could apply bandages, Blanche was forced to put her finger in the wound to stop the bleeding. "Due to the lack of medical attention," an interrogator later noted, "the wound in Barrow's head gave off such an offensive odor that it was with utmost difficulty that one could remain within several feet of him." Buck was in such dire condition that Clyde was prepared to drive him all the way to their mother's home in Texas. He and Buck had promised each other that if either brother was ever mortally wounded or killed, the other brother would bring him home to her if they were able to do so.

On July 23rd, about three days after they had arrived, the group left to buy some medical supplies & food, leaving the campsite for a few hours. A local person found evidence suggesting that someone had burned some bloody bandages. He had heard the radio reports telling of the possibility of wounded fugitives being in the area and called Town Marshal John Love. Love then contacted Dallas County Sheriff C.A. Knee in Adel.

There are different versions of who this local person, that first discovered the campsite, was. One account claimed that it was a person by the name of Ed Penn, who had been taking a stroll through the park. Another account purports that a man named Henry Nye, out hunting wild blackberries on his property, came across the camp. Actually, the first to discover the camp was a troop of fourteen Girl Scouts led by Della Gowdey, who were camping at the old pavilion of the park. They took an early morning hike and walked right into the Barrow Gang campsite. Maxine Schell Hadley, a member of this troop, said the campers acted quite surprised. She had no idea who they were. Della and the other girls said good morning. Maxine remembered the campers smiled and returned the welcome. Maxine thought nothing

Chapter Thirteen: Bonnie and Clyde at Dexter

about it until the next day when she saw two people in Dexter whom she had seen at the campground. The man was eating an ice cream cone and the lady had none. She thought it was very discourteous of the man not to offer the lady some ice cream as well. These two people were probably Bonnie and Clyde.

Sheriff Knee didn't take any chances, as he had a pretty good idea who he would be dealing with. He quickly formed a posse, which included Des Moines police officers and detectives, a Des Moines dentist, Dr. Hershel Keller, who was also a National Guardsman, and many locals. They swore in a couple of new deputies and located every farmer or storekeeper who owned even a squirrel gun or pistol. Dr. Keller even brought his own machine gun. The posse totaled about 50 people.

They surrounded the campsite and took up their positions in the nearby bushes. By late afternoon, two cars returned to the campsite, one of them bearing several bullet holes. The posse remained in the bushes through the night watching their prey.

That same night, the gang made their camp beside the two cars. W.D. kept busy inspecting the damage to the vehicles and transferring equipment to the stolen Ford. He also removed ammunition from a great many pasteboard boxes and stored it in an old innertube, which he put behind the seat of the Ford. Clyde busied himself meticulously cleaning their weapons and Bonnie nursed her burned legs without the medicine that was left in Platte City, and tried to sleep.

Early the next morning, they threw caution to the wind and made a campfire to fix breakfast. While W.D. cooked some sausages, Bonnie was busy brewing the coffee. Suddenly a shout echoed through the timber. That shout was the beginning of the famous Dexfield Park shootout.

"This is the law! Come out here!" boomed through the trees.

"Get the hell out of here, you sons-a-bitches! We'll kill you!" Clyde screamed back as he grabbed a Browning Automatic Rifle and started shooting. Suddenly gunfire erupted from the bushes surrounding the camp. Bonnie screamed as every one of them started grabbing for their weapons, even Blanche.

W.D did not even have time to straighten up from the campfire before bullets started flying. As he tried to run to the car, he was struck by a load of buckshot to the face and chest. Two slugs also struck him, one in the calf of his left leg and the other in his upper right chest.

Clyde was struck in the head by a ricocheting bullet, which temporarily stunned him. Quickly recovering, he jumped behind the wheel of one of the cars and put it into gear. He began to drive the car to where the others had been waiting. Just then a bullet struck him in the arm causing him to drive onto a tree stump. With this car disabled, Clyde and W.D. Jones ran to the other car, only to see it disabled and almost reduced to rubble by the onslaught of gunfire. Bonnie, Clyde, and W.D. Jones took off, leaving Blanche and Buck. Everyone in the gang had been wounded except Blanche.

Bonnie, Clyde, and W.D went east and then north towards the South Raccoon River. Clyde tried to go back to the road through the old amusement park. He was met by two members of the posse: Deputy Evan Burger and the editor of the Dexter Sentinel, Everett Place. He exchanged gunfire with them and went back to Bonnie and W.D. Together they crossed the river and worked their way behind Spillers Cemetery. They were all wounded and losing blood. The timber along the river was second growth but it was dense, creating a problem for the lawmen pursuing the three.

"We weren't very organized when we went after them," John Love would later remark. "They were up the hill from the park and I'd never really been out there. I thought Sheriff Clint Knee was in charge until I found out he had turned it over to the Iowa state department. After it was all over, the next day, if someone had yelled scat, I probably would have shot them. That's the way I felt."

After crossing the river, Bonnie, Clyde and W.D. came upon the farmstead of Vallie Feller. Clyde left Bonnie and W.D and approached the farmstead, hoping to steal a car. Vallie Feller, his son

Chapter Thirteen: Bonnie and Clyde at Dexter

Marvelle, and hired man Walt Spillers had heard the gunshots and wondered what was going on. They were on their way to milk the cows when they saw a small bloodied man walk out of the cornfield. Clyde Barrow pointed a .45 caliber revolver at them.

As the Feller's dog barked and bounded toward him, Clyde told them to pull off the dog or he would kill, it. He then told them he needed help. He whistled and W.D. came up the fence carrying Bonnie. As Marvelle and Vallie helped lift her over the fence, Vallie dropped her. Clyde was quite irritated by this and told them to hold on to her. He next told them he needed a car. The Fellers had three cars on the place but no money for fuel. The only car that was running was the Feller family car: a blue 1929 Plymouth. During this exchange, Marvelle's mother and nine-year-old sister came out of the house to see if the men knew anything about all the shooting going on. She walked right into the rest of her family being held at gunpoint by Clyde and became quite excited and very upset. Clyde told Vallie to settle her down. He said, "the laws are shooting the hell out of us and all we need is the car to get out of here."

Bonnie and W.D. Jones got into the back seat of the car and Clyde got into the driver's seat. The car started right up, but Clyde had never driven a Plymouth, and Marvelle had to show him how to shift the gears. Clyde thanked Marvelle for all their help and said he would pay them back someday. For a long time afterwards, the authorities censored the Feller mail, but nothing ever arrived. It is interesting to note that after W.D. Jones was captured and confessed, he said Clyde was out of ammunition when he confronted the Feller family that day. Marvelle said he thought he could have taken them on but did not want to risk Clyde testing his .45 caliber revolver on him.

During the initial gunfight, Buck had received a gunshot wound in his back (it has been reported he may have received as many as five gunshot wounds to his back). He was on the ground, but Blanche refused to leave him. As the lawmen closed in, Blanche somehow got Buck into the clearing where the baseball diamond had been. Near that clearing was a large tree that had apparently been cut down by the WPA loggers. They took refuge behind the log.

The posse tracking Buck and Blanche had organized at the campsite shortly after the gunfight. Sheriff Knee told them they should start looking for bodies in the underbrush as the fugitives had been hit by gunfire. The volunteers divided into groups, one of which was manned by Kirt Piper and about five others. This group went up a steep hill and down a bank where they came upon heel marks sunk deep into the dirt. They followed these marks and came upon a flat open area with a large tree that had been felled nearby. Piper thought the felled tree would be a good place to hide and had the others slowly approach it. Suddenly Blanche stood up from behind the tree. Piper said she was wearing "riding breeches, a pair of nice boots, sunglasses and she didn't look too clean."

"My husband is on the ground and he can't move," Blanche screamed.

The posse demanded he get up and asked if he was armed. Blanche did not answer. Holding on to her husband, she began crying out to them. "Stop, don't shoot! He's already dying." Piper said through it all she was pretty hysterical.

As Buck was laying there on the ground, a member of the posse mashed his throat with his boot and stuck a shotgun in his face. "I thought that was a little too much and unnecessary," a bystander quipped.

Kirt Piper explains what happened next. "Buck Barrow was finally coaxed to his feet. He would walk for a ways, then he would collapse. The posse would drag him a few feet and then he would get his feet under him and he would walk a little ways. Buck had a bad pallor, a ghastly-looking pallor, his head wound was not bandaged…his brains were exposed, and you could tell this man was on his last legs."

About a quarter mile from where Buck and Blanche were captured, Des Moines Register photographer Herb Schwartz took the famous photograph of Blanche being held by Sheriff Loren Forbes.

Chapter Thirteen: Bonnie and Clyde at Dexter

Blanche is struggling with Forbes and looking directly at the camera and screaming. In his notes, Schwartz explains that in her semi-blind state, Blanche saw him raise his camera and thought it was a gun and I was about to shoot Buck. She had been somewhat subdued up until that time.

Buck Barrow, what was left of him, was taken to Chapler-Osborne Clinic in Dexter, along with Blanche. Blanche Barrow had been suffering from shards of glass that were embedded in her eye after the Platte City shootout. Dr. Clyde and Nurse Bonnie had attempted to remove a large piece of glass using a pair of tweezers. That attempt failed, as the tweezers kept slipping off.

While at the clinic, Blanch made an attempt to escape. When she was taken to the examining room, she asked to go to the bathroom. A nurse had her remove all her clothes and put on a hospital gown and wrap a sheet around herself. She was then led by the nurse to the bathroom, which was in the basement of the clinic. As she reached the landing, Blanche spotted a door that led to the alley outside. She tried to make a break for the door and struggled with the much larger nurse who held on tight. Officers soon arrived and Blanche was subdued.

Subduing Blanche would not have been a monumental task. Her weight was listed as 81 pounds, down 33 ½ pounds from January. She was a small woman to begin with and had lost a considerable amount of weight while on the run. That form of weight loss is not recommended, however.

The doctors decided to transport Buck to King's Daughter Hospital in Perry, 28 miles away, so they could operate on him. They were afraid that the crowds might pose a problem, so they devised an ingenious plan. An officer with a bullhorn stood at the front door of the Chapler-Osborne Clinic and announced that a call from a reliable source had just come in stating that Bonnie and Clyde were on their way to Dexter to free Buck Barrow. Within minutes, the streets were cleared. Dr. Chapler observed that "you could have shot a cannon down Main Street and never touched a soul."

After stealing the Plymouth from the Feller farm, Bonnie, Clyde and W.D. Jones drove to Polk City, 38 miles northeast of Dexter. Somehow, they managed to wreck the bloodstained and battered car and left it there. In need of wheels, and apparently more dough, they held up a gas station and stole the attendant's car. One account of where they went after that has them fleeing to Guthrie Center, which would have been about 45 miles in the opposite direction they had just come from. There they were supposedly spotted and surrounded by 200 men in a posse. With Clyde using his well-practiced driving skills, they managed to escape once again. The trio was reportedly last seen about 60 miles northeast of Sioux City. The car they had stolen in Polk City was found abandoned, also bloodstained, in Broken Bow, Nebraska.

W.D. Jones eventually left the gang and went back to Texas. A co-worker there turned him in to the police and he served time in prison for his role with the Barrow Gang. Bonnie and Clyde had escaped this time, but the shoot-out in Iowa was the beginning of the end for them. In less than a year, on May 23, 1934, they were ambushed and killed in Gibsland, Louisiana. Bonnie and Clyde may have died, but the "Legend of Bonnie and Clyde" continues to this day.

Buck arrived at King's Daughter Hospital in Perry by ambulance and was put in a private room under guard. He was said to be generally lucid when admitted. He told doctors that aspirin helped the pain in his head and the only real pain he felt was from his other gunshot wounds, particularly the one in his back. The doctors determined that the bullet had entered his back, ricocheted off a rib and lodged in his chest wall close to the pleural cavity. His limbs were paralyzed from another bullet wound and his temperature would not lower from 105. His doctors were not very optimistic for any recovery. They expected he would develop pneumonia from the surgery on his chest because he was in such a weakened state, or infection of his brain from the head wound would kill him in a few days.

During Buck's stay at the hospital, the doors were barred, and the place was surrounded by armed lawmen. There were fears that

Chapter Thirteen: Bonnie and Clyde at Dexter

Clyde and Bonnie would attempt to get Buck out of police custody. Only the doctors and nurses were allowed to enter the premises.

When lawmen visited him in the hospital to get his final statements, the doctors helped enable Buck to chat with them. They had kept him numb with opiates, but they also injected him with stimulants at least twice, so that he might answer questions.

Once again, Buck's stinky fragrance was noted by one of the interrogators who stated, "Due to the lack of medical attention, the wound in Barrow's head gave off such an offensive odor that it was with utmost difficulty that one could remain within several feet of him." A curious doctor got close enough to ask Buck "Where are you wanted by the law?"

"Wherever I've been," Buck replied.

The sheriff of the other Dallas County, the one in Texas, Sheriff R.A."Smoot" Schmid, wrote a letter of introduction to the local authorities for Buck and Clyde's mother, Cumie. A sympathetic deputy sheriff provided money to help her cover the costs of the 36-hour drive to Iowa. Emma Parker and her daughter Billie had also gone to the Perry, Iowa hospital along with Cumie and her youngest son, Leon C. Barrow. While there, they rented rooms in a house that was located directly across the street from the hospital. The Texas contingent arrived in time for Buck's last conscious days. As his pneumonia strengthened, he became delirious and finally slipped into a coma, from which he did not wake. True to the sawbone's predictions, Buck Barrow died at 2 p.m. on July 29, 1933, five days after his final shootout.

Blanche was taken from the clinic in Dexter to Adel. Later that same day, she was transferred to Polk County Jail in Des Moines. From Des Moines, she was sent to Platte County, Missouri where she was charged with attempting to murder Sheriff Coffey in the Platte City shootout. Blanche said she found Coffey remarkably sympathetic but wasn't so generous in describing J. Edgar Hoover. She claimed that while interrogating her, Hoover had threatened to gouge out her remaining good eye.

Blanch Barrow was found guilty of attempting to murder Sheriff Coffey and sentenced to ten years in the Missouri State Prison in Jefferson City. Blanche had at least four operations on her eye while in the Missouri prison. She was paroled after six years. During her time in prison, as well as after her parole, she remained in close contact with Coffey and his family and Platte County prosecutor David Clevenger. Blanche moved to Dallas, Texas, after serving her sentence, and worked at several different jobs. In 1940, she married Eddie Frasure. One year later, she completed her two-year parole, but police continued to monitor her. In later life she said Bonnie and Clyde seemed like characters in a book she had read. Eddie died in 1969 and Blanche died from cancer in 1988, aged 77. At the time, she was survived by her 93-year-old mother. She was buried in Dallas' Grove Hill Memorial Park as Blanche B. Frasure.

Bonnie and Clyde returned to Iowa frequently following the Dexter raid and robbed at least four banks in the state: Rembrandt on January 23, Knierim on February 1, Stuart on April 16 and Everly on May 3rd.

The gang went back to Texas in September of 1933 to see their families. W.D Jones continued on to Houston where his mother had moved. On November 16, he was arrested there without incident and returned to Dallas. At his trial the following October, all state witnesses recommended against the death penalty. Jones was convicted of murder without malice on October 12. The jury handed down a sentence of fifteen years, although the district attorney and the prosecuting attorney both recommended a sentence of 99 years. In February of 1935, the federal government tried a test case on the charge of "harboring" against Jones and nineteen other family members and associates of Barrow and Parker. Jones received the maximum sentence for harboring, two years, applied to run concurrently with his Texas sentence. After six years residing in the Huntsville Texas Penitentiary, W.D. Jones was paroled. The six years Blanche Barrow served was the same time as W.D Jones, who had killed several people.

Chapter Thirteen: Bonnie and Clyde at Dexter

Clyde Barrow committed several robberies that fall, while his family, and Bonnie Parker's, attended to her burns and other medical needs. On November 22, Dallas Sherriff Smoot Schmid, Deputy Bob Alcorn, and Deputy Ted Hinton set up an ambush for Bonnie and Clyde while they were trying to meet with family members near Sowers, Texas. The lawmen lay in wait nearby as Barrow drove up. He sensed the trap, however, and drove past his family's car. Schmid and his deputies stood up and opened fire with machine guns and a Browning Automatic Rifle. One bullet passed through the car, striking the legs of both Barrow and Parker. They escaped later that night.

Bonnie and Clyde met their end on May 23, 1934, on a rural road in Bienville Parish, Louisiana. Texas officers Frank Hamer, B.M. Gault, Bob Alcorn, and Ted Hinton, and Louisiana officers Henderson Jordan and Prentiss Morel Oakley formed the posse. Hamer, who led the posse, had begun tracking them. On May 21, the four posse members from Texas were in Shreveport, Louisiana when they learned that Barrow and Parker were to go to Bienville Parish that evening with Henry Methvin, a 22-year-old criminal who had replaced W.D. Jones. Methvin had gotten separated from them in Shreveport and Clyde had designated the residence of Methvin's parents as a rendezvous in case they were separated. The full posse set up an ambush at the rendezvous point along Louisiana State Highway 154 south of Gibsland toward Sailes. They were in place by 9 p.m. and waited through all of the next day with no sign of the famous gang.

It was approximately 9:15, on the morning of May 23, that their patience was finally rewarded. Still concealed in the bushes and almost ready to concede defeat, they finally heard Barrow's stolen 1934 Ford V8 approaching at a high speed. Their official report had Barrow stopping to speak with Methvin's father, who had been planted there with his truck that morning to distract Barrow and force him into the lane closer to the posse.

The lawmen opened fire, shooting about 130 rounds into the car. Oakley fired first, probably before any order to do so. Clyde Barrow was killed instantly by Oakley's head shot. Hinton reported hearing Parker scream as she realized that Barrow was dead, just as they began shooting in her direction. The officers emptied all their weapons at the car. Nearly any of their wounds would have been fatal, yet the two had survived many bullets over the years in their confrontations with the law.

To give you an idea of the firepower involved, each of six officers had a shotgun, an automatic rifle and pistols. They emptied the automatic rifles first, then they used shotguns. After shooting the shotguns, they emptied the pistols at the car. By that time, the car had passed them and ran into a ditch about 50 yards away. "It almost turned over," one of the lawmen reported. "We kept shooting at the car even after it stopped. We weren't taking any chances."

Undertaker C.F. "Boots" Bailey had difficulty embalming the bodies because of all the bullet holes. Just imagine pumping embalming fluid into a body and having it pour out everywhere, like water from a sieve.

When she wasn't robbing banks, Bonnie wrote poetry. Her best-known composition is titled "The Story of Bonnie and Clyde"

> *Someday they'll go down together;*
> *And they'll bury them side by side;*
> *To few it'll be grief*
> *To the law a relief*
> *But it's death for Bonnie and Clyde*

The shootout in Dallas County was the beginning of the end for Bonnie and Clyde.

Chapter Thirteen: Bonnie and Clyde at Dexter

The Capture of Blanche Barrow

Wounded Buck Barrow (On Ground)

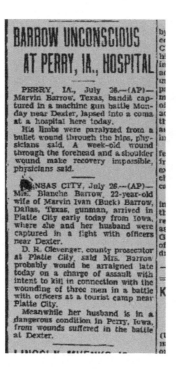

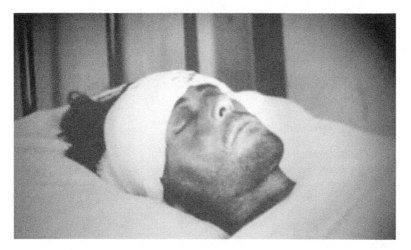

Buck Barrow at King's Daughter Hospital

Chapter Thirteen: Bonnie and Clyde at Dexter

King's Daughter Hospital at Perry

Bonnie and Clyde

Chapter Fourteen

The Dirty Thirty's

Dallas County was not immune from The Great Depression, which lasted from 1929 to 1939. 1933 was the worst year of the depression with unemployment peaking at 25.2%. One in four people were unemployed. It was also the year that Adolf Hitler became the chancellor of Germany and opened the first concentration camp at Dachau. There was a panic of people withdrawing their money from banks and the US banking system had to be propped up by the US government (US banking act of 1933). The continuing drought in the Midwest made even more of the land into dust bowls. Thousands of men traveled the roads and rails in America looking for work. Nowhere in Dallas County was this more evident than in Perry, a railroad town.

These conditions helped create an unprecedented crime wave. Perhaps the most famous gangster of the previous decade was Al Capone, an organized crime boss in Chicago. He became rich providing illegal alcohol during prohibition. It's not surprising that many people of that time thought of Capone as a "Robin Hood" type figure because he gave to charities and helped the poor. It's true that he did indeed start one of the first soup kitchens to feed the unemployed in Chicago, but he was also responsible for the deaths of at least 33 people. Capone was sent to federal prison in 1932 for tax evasion.

Chapter Fourteen: The Dirty Thirty's

John Dillinger was a famous bank robber during the Great Depression. Many people also looked at him as more of a hero than a villain because he mostly robbed banks and banks were about as popular during the depression as a porcupine at a nudist camp. Dillinger and his gang robbed at least 24 banks before 1934, when a woman in red smiled on him and he was gunned down in Chicago.

Other famous Depression-era criminals, besides Bonnie and Clyde, included Pretty Boy Floyd, Baby Face Nelson, Baron Lamm, and Slick Willie Sutton.

The best-known brush with big-time Depression-Era criminals in Dallas County was the Bonnie and Clyde Dexfield shootout. But there were many small-time criminals preying on the struggling citizens. Here's a few stories from that difficult time.

February 3, 1931…John Smith

John Smith of Perry was a well-known manufacturer of a stock and poultry insecticide called Disintone. The business did well, making great growth in a short time. Smith was so successful that he had even run for governor of Iowa on the Farmer Labor ticket.

On the evening of February 3, 1931, he left Perry with a truckload of Disintone destined for the western part of the state. Near Dennison, the truck ran into the ditch and caught fire. A passing motorist attempted, but failed, to rescue the driver from the burning truck. When it was finally removed, the body was burned beyond recognition. The family had the charred body taken to Perry for burial.

A short time before this unfortunate accident, Smith had taken out a large amount of life insurance. When his wife tried to collect $10,000 on one of his policies, the insurance company immediately became suspicious and refused payment.

After looking into the incident further, they became even more suspicious. On March 12, 1931, the body was exhumed, and it was proved beyond doubt that it was not the body of John Smith.

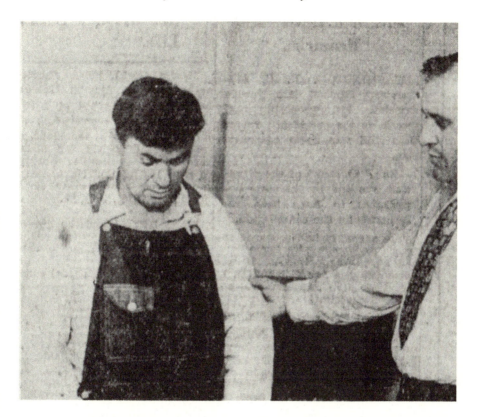

John M. Smith being held by Sheriff Knee

Immediately, a statewide search began for Smith. The case baffled officers for several months. In St Paul Mn., he bought a new car. On April 11th, he married Miss Pauline Shaw in Kansas. Later, his wife received a tip to meet him at a certain time at Blacks Corner. Officers accompanied her to this place and although they recognized him, failed to capture the mysterious criminal. For weeks, nothing further was heard of him. Not only was the matter the subject of conversation throughout Iowa, but newspapers as far away as California devoted whole columns to the story. During some of the high spots of the case, newspaper reporters came to Perry from Omaha Saint Paul and other cities. On the morning of June 23rd, a farmer near

Chapter Fourteen: The Dirty Thirty's

Garner, Iowa found a man bound with wire, hand and foot, along the roadside. The man, who said he had been robbed and kidnapped, proved to be Smith. He was returned to Perry, and then to Adel, where he pleaded insanity. Judge W.S. Cooper committed him to the department for criminally insane at the Anamosa Penitentiary. Six years later, May 17 of 1937, he was declared sane by the Iowa Sanity Commission, and returned to Sheriff knee at Adel.

I was not able to determine what became of Smith after being returned to Dallas County. Trying to find information on someone named John Smith is like trying to find an honest man in congress. You would have to do a lot of lookin'.

December 21, 1934…Yeggs Blast Open Safes in Two Places

What in the Sam Hill is a Yegg? Well, for those who don't know, here's the dictionary definition: *"Yegg…a burglar or safecracker."*

The "Yeggs," in this story, were Gerald Duffy, Charles Bales, Max Botsford and Ed Fletcher, all of Des Moines. They must have been looking for some extra holiday gift money when they burglarized eight establishments in Adel and Waukee, on a Thursday night just four days before Christmas. The next morning, Friday, several unsuspecting merchants opened their doors for the day's business and received quite a shock. The mischief included two one-ton safes that were blasted open and two others that were unlocked and ransacked, along with a lot of other mayhem.

"The heaviest haul was taken at the Morril Drug Store in Waukee," according to reporter Herbert Owens of the Des Moines Tribune. In addition to $5 cash, the thieves also got away with the narcotics from an open safe and swept the most valuable merchandise from the shelves. The list of the "valuable merchandise" includes seventy-two fountain pens and pencils, a clock, four watches, a leather handbag, three dresser sets and a smoking set.

Murder and Mayhem in Dallas County

At the Brenton Lumber Co, also in Waukee, the thieves hauled in $70 cash from a huge safe, which was blasted. The heavy door of the safe was blown to bits by the explosion. Entry was through a window directly above the safe.

The Yeggs wasted a lot of time jimmying a door open at the Waukee Railroad Elevator, just off the main highway. The elevator had not been in operation and there was no loot to be had.

At the Farmer's Elevator Co, they did just slightly better than nothing. They obtained, for their efforts, a small radio and a lantern flashlight. No "clews" (there's that word again) were obtained from any of these burglaries.

Their next target, the Elder and Law Oil Station and Lunchroom, did provide some "clews." Attendants reported that the previous day, three customers aroused suspicion. The three entered the lunchroom and while one ordered a cup of coffee, the others spent much time in the backroom under the pretense of using the lavatory. Friday morning, F.O. Elder, one of the proprietors, found the rear window open and the place ransacked. Elder reported a radio, cash register, a supply of cigarettes and tobacco and ten gallons of oil in two cans were taken. The thieves must have worked up an appetite by this time as several large packages of cookies were also missing.

The Yeggs didn't end up with near as much profit when they moved on west to Adel. At the local Ford dealer, Mitchell Motor Co., the thieves entered through a window in the rear garage. They wheeled a new one-ton safe from under a night light in the showroom to an inner office where it was blasted. Approximately $35 was taken. Golden Mitchell, proprietor, said he had banked $100 late Thursday, the day before the burglary. Papers and private records were scattered throughout the office by the blast. The thieves unlatched the main garage door from the inside to make their escape.

Two dollars was taken from an unlocked safe in the office of the Eclipse Lumber Co. and $1 in cash and $1 in stamps was the only loot from the Verne Danielson Elevator Co.

Chapter Fourteen: The Dirty Thirty's

Sheriff C.A. Knee and his deputies visited the places Friday but said they were without "clews." (OK, I did a little research on clue vs clew and maybe, just maybe, we can give the reporters a little leeway. Here's the information from Grammarist: *A clue is a hint or a piece of evidence that aids one in coming to a conclusion concerning a crime or a mystery. Interestingly, the word clue is derived from the word clew. The word "clue," as in "a piece of evidence used as a guide in solving a mystery or a problem," originally means "a ball of thread," and it was spelled "clew." What's thread got to do with clues? The answer is in the story of Ariadne, Theseus and the Minotaur. In Greek mythology the Minotaur is a violent monster, half human and half bull, born on the island of Crete. To keep it from hurting people, the king of the island makes Daedalus, an inventor and architect, create a labyrinth that the Minotaur will never be able to escape.*

If you want more information on this fascinating subject, look it up. Getting back to the story of the Yeggs, the four men were caught and sentenced in February to 40 years in prison. Duffy was sentenced to Anamosa reformatory and Botsford and Bales were sent to Fort Madison.

Burglarizing and safecracking on cold Iowa nights had apparently caused Ed Fletcher to come down with a case of pneumonia, so his trial had to be postponed to April. Max Botsford, who had the weight of 25 other robberies on his record before he was finally sent "down the river," was brought back from Fort Madison to testify. That turned out to be a big mistake. On his return back to the "big house" after the trial, Botsford decided he liked it better on the outside and the first chance he got he ran for the hills.

Actually, he eluded Dallas County Deputy Sheriff E.A. Burger (who would later become Sheriff Evan A. Burger) at the Des Moines Wig-Wam barbecue on East Fourteenth Street north of Euclid. The restaurant was operated by Botsford's father, whom he was allowed to stop and visit on his way back to the penitentiary. That wasn't the only stop that Botsford was allowed. Previous to that, he was taken to the home of a girlfriend in Des Moines to say goodbye to her. You would think he would have said his goodbyes when he was originally sent to Fort Madison in February. While leaving the barbeque, Botsford asked to step in the shadow for a moment (I think this means he told Burger he needed to pee). When a minute or two went by and he did not return, the escape was discovered. This sounds to me like one of the oldest tricks in the book. I can't believe Burger fell for it.

The next day, Botsford surrendered at a schoolhouse north of the Des Moines city limits near the Wig-Wam Barbeque where he had escaped. This time, he was taken straight to Fort Madison.

In case you haven't been keeping track, here's the total haul for this band of "Yeggs," $140 in cash, two radios and a flashlight, a cash register, $300 worth of pencils and pens and other drug store merchandise and $35 worth of narcotics. Split that four ways and you have to ask yourself, "Was it worth it?" Four men had many years in prison to ponder that.

Golden Mitchell Looks Over the Damage

Chapter Fourteen: The Dirty Thirty's

June 18, 1935…Adel's Mayor and Doctor Busted on Narcotics Charge

Adel Mayor W.D. Valentine and Adel Doctor C.E. Mershon were arraigned on a narcotics charge. They both pleaded not guilty to two complaints, one charging violation of the Harrison Narcotic Law and the other charging a conspiracy to violate it. They were held for a preliminary hearing to determine if evidence against them was sufficient to warrant grand jury action. Bond for each man was set at $5,000 by United States Commissioner John R. Hamilton. Efforts were made by friends to meet the surety.

William E. Clark of Minneapolis, Minn., district supervisor of federal narcotic agents, had directed his officers in Iowa to make the investigation. Agents said that they had reports of a "half dozen" Iowa towns where physicians and town officials were co-operating in the illegal sale of narcotics.

Narcotic addicts, who went to Adel in a search for drugs, were told by Dr. Mershon that he could not supply them unless they had a written order from Mayor Valentine. The mayor charged these addicts $2 for these orders, the government claims. In a sting operation, undercover workers, employed by Narcotic Agents W.D. Morris of Des Moines and Pat O'Leary of Minneapolis, made 14 purchases of morphine and cocaine from Dr. Mershon, it was charged. In each instance, they were first required to obtain a written order from Mayor Valentine.

Following their arrest, the mayor and doctor declared they were after a bunch of gangsters. "Whatever we did, we thought we did lawfully," said Mayor Valentine, who spoke for the two. "We were after a bunch of gangsters, at least four of them, and I guess we were just too slow. We should have arrested them as we could, but I wanted Dillon to get the bunch." Dillon, he said, is Archie Dillon, Adel town marshal.

The mayor also said the purchasers were with two other men and he spoke of a woman. "We intended to arrest them all," he said "all at once. And here they turned out to be federal stool pigeons. I don't suppose we'll have much chance of convincing the federal men of that," he added "but we're certainly going to try. Ignorance of the law, I guess they say, excuses no one."

The mayor was dressed in overalls. He was a blacksmith and had been mayor for two years. Dr. Mershon, who was dressed in white shoes, gray trousers, and white shirt, said he was a cousin of Municipal Judge J.E. Mershon of Des Moines.

The arraignment of Valentine and Dr. Mershon came before some 12 or 15 Adel residents, who had come to the federal building to visit their mayor and the physician. Many of the visitors expressed confidence in the two men and a belief they would be cleared. Representing the men at the arraignment were John G. Regan, city attorney of Adel, and Attorneys R.K. Craft of Adel and Wendell Huston of Des Moines.

Federal narcotics agents who worked on the case said the law states that doctors can dispense narcotics only to bona-fide patients in the course of professional practice and good faith. "There seems to be some mistaken notions about this law," one agent said. "A druggist is also held equally liable with a doctor in the dispensing of narcotics and both men must keep records of all such drugs they dispense."

Both men were freed on bond and a preliminary hearing was set for July 2. At that time, they waived the preliminary hearing and their bond was continued. No further information was available on this incident, other than W.D. Valentine was reelected mayor at the next city election and Dr. Mershon continued as a Physician for many years afterwards.

This incident happened at the depths of the depression. We will probably never know if the story the two men gave about trying to catch drug addicts is true or they were just trying to make a few bucks. Considering the times, who could blame them if it was the latter.

Chapter Fourteen: The Dirty Thirty's

Mayor W. D. Valentine, foreground, and Dr. C. E. Mershon, both of Adel, Ia., as they appeared at the Polk county jail Monday night awaiting arraignment today on charges of violating federal narcotic laws.

Murder and Mayhem in Dallas County

May 28, 1937...Iowa Bureau Hears from New Agent.

A Des Moines man, who was being held in Atlantic Iowa, presented The Iowa Bureau of Investigation with a mystery problem. The man, who apparently believed he was one of the bureau's agents, faced a charge of robbing the George McGinnis gasoline station in Adel, Iowa. He also was detained for impersonating an officer.

The first word to the Bureau was this wire from the man, received by W.W. Akers, Bureau Chief:

Stopped 18 cars and 5 trucks since called this morning. I'm reporting from Atlantic. Have a hunch to leave immediately for red Oak and play cautiously from there into Council Bluffs. Wire me any information care Chieftain Hotel Council Bluffs. Have checked on every oil station at every camp on Hwy 6.

The telegram came collect.

Atlantic officials said the man related that he had met a group of soldiers in a beer tavern in Des Moines and that they had commissioned him to take the job. Sheriff C.A. Knee of Adel said he would file a charge against the man unless he is found to be insane. He was in the custody of Sheriff P.P. Edwards of Atlantic.

Where was the George McGinnis Gasoline Station in Adel, you may wonder? It was at the corner of Greene, which was highway 6 at the time, and 14th Street. If you're still not sure, I've added a picture on the next page.

Chapter Fourteen: The Dirty Thirty's

McGinnis Gasoline Station - Better Known as Clancy's Motor Court

Chapter Fifteen

Mystery Skull

The old Graney Bridge, that once crossed the North Raccoon River south of Perry, has been gone for many years. The wrought iron bridge with overhead trusses was typical of bridges constructed before the turn of the century. It has been replaced by a modern steel and concrete structure that spans the river along County Highway P-58. But the old bridge is not forgotten. Something strange happened at the old Graney Bridge 90 years ago, and the mystery remains unsolved to this day.

The early morning hours of Saturday November 28, 1931 were cold and snowy. Bert Bailey, along with his 16-year-old son Leon and Leon's friend, 14-year-old Paul Black, were out coon hunting with Leon's dog Storm. A little after midnight, while waiting for Storm to come back from a hunting trip through the woods, they witnessed a strange sight. Sitting in their parked car at the west approach to the bridge, just off the road, a light coupe passed within three feet of their car and drove into the bridge. They heard a noise they described as "sort of a crack." The three left their car and started towards the bridge, fearing the coupe had struck their dog or that the car had gone through the bridge railing into the River. As they approached the bridge, they could make out the dim forms of two men walking toward them lugging a bundle, which appeared to be the size of a human body. They had parked their car across the bridge from Bert Baileys house.

Chapter Fifteen: Mystery Skull

As the three stood there peering through the fog and light snow, they saw the men halt beside the bridge rail. The three heard a splash in the Raccoon that echoed and re-echoed. The startled hunters rushed back to their own car and started away. Nearly at the same time, the two men in the coupe roared away into the darkness. The car ahead had gone several hundred yards before it's lights were turned on. The actions of its occupants indicated they were unaware of the presence of witnesses. Bailey, Leon and Paul Black attempted to follow the coupe but lost them in the darkness.

When Bailey investigated the scene the next morning after the incident, he made a startling discovery, blood on the bridge railing. He notified authorities. The County Sheriff's Department took charge and began an investigation.

Dragging in the River was begun at 10:30 a.m. Sunday at the bridge, with county officers in charge. Using a power boat manned by the Payne Brothers of Adel, the workers combed the river in the vicinity of the bridge and also made a tour of inspection downstream before dinner. In the afternoon, while several thousand people watched from the bridge and surrounding banks, an even more concentrated search was made for the body. A rope was stretched across the stream and the men who were dragging used bamboo poles with hooks attached. The purpose of the rope was to enable them to hold the boat steadier than was possible with the outboard motor. The stream was dragged all day Sunday, but no evidence of a possible crime was discovered.

Further mystery was added when Ruphus Bennick, a farmer residing seven miles south and a mile and a half west of Dawson, reported that a farmhand employed by Elmer Snively, his neighbor, had disappeared on November 28th, the night of the strange happening on the bridge. Bennick said that the farmhand was last seen near the Square Deal Grocery Store in Perry. He quoted the farmhand as saying he was returning to a gambling game in which he had won some money earlier in the evening. Two other unidentified men were with Snively's farmhand, Bennick said. He further stated the three men were last seen at approximately 10 p.m. The hand, William Rufus Danforth, was said to be 45 years-old and was wearing overalls and a cap.

The search continued the following Monday. Searchers met at Minburn and took the boat to the place where the hunt had halted Sunday night. They skimmed down the stream and planned to continue on down as far as the Adel dam if necessary. In the boat were Sheriff Clint A. Knee, Lloyd Roland and Willard and Joe Payne of Adel, owners of the power boat. The search had been resumed at the request of the County Board of Supervisors, but searchers had only vague clues to encourage them.

Sheriff Knee was beginning to have doubts that a body had actually been tossed into the water. The searchers, on Sunday, had found a bushel basket of animal entrails and a sheep pelt a quarter of a mile downstream from the Graney Bridge. This led Sheriff Knee to the belief that someone had been butchering and had thrown the basket over the bridge railing. The viscera were taken by Sheriff knee to be submitted to a veterinarian for further examination. Dragging operations were ceased Monday night.

A sample of the blood from the railing was sent to the State University of Iowa where the dean of the pharmacy college, W.J. Teeters, examined it. Teeters said that as far as he could determine the blood is that of a human. In a telephone conversation, he said that he would not swear the blood is that of a human but that the sign of the red corpuscles indicated that it was from a goat, monkey or human. Teeters added, "there is no doubt in my mind that the blood was from a human being's body."

The mystery deepened when authorities established that William Danforth, missing farmhand, was seen November 30th, the day following the occurrence at the bridge that had prompted the investigation. County officers learned that Danforth lost about $35 in a dice game the night of November 28th.

Snively said that he, his wife Eva, their ten-year-old daughter Mary and Danforth all went into Perry Saturday for a night on the town.

Chapter Fifteen: Mystery Skull

They were to meet at a grocery store at ten o'clock to return home. Shortly after ten, Danforth came to their car and told them he was in a big card game, was winning, and would be home later. "That was the last we saw or heard of him," Snively added.

Three transients, one of whom was Danforth, were reported gambling for big money at a grocery store that night, and one of the participants won big. The other men involved in the game were never identified.

It was also reported that Danforth was seen at the home of Pearl MacGill, Negro girl, the next night. Robert Langfitt, local blacksmith, said that he accompanied Danforth to Miss McGill's home on the night in question.

In an effort to throw more light on the farmhand's whereabouts, authorities raided Harry's Used Cars, operated by Harry Oppinheim. Several other men, also in the place, were questioned but none was held (I haven't been able to establish the connection between Oppinheim and Danforth but possibly he was a known gambler, and this is where the game took place instead of a grocery store).

In recounting the history of his hired man, Snively said that Slim Danforth came to his farm about the second week in October from Bagley, where he had been camping out. "He was a good hand," Snively said, "who always did his work well. He played with the kids and showed them a rosary that he carried. He was devoutly religious." Danforth had told him he spent more than 10 years in the army and had showed him his service papers which, with a picture or two of himself, that he always carried on his person. His only other known personal effects were the articles found in his room at the farmhouse after his disappearance. Despite the fact that Danforth left a parcel containing a prayer book, some cheap rings and some clothing at the Snively home before he left there for the last time November 28th, the Sheriff said that Danforth might have returned to his Indiana home. Danforth's hometown is thought to be Crosby, Indiana, Snively said.

Deputy Tom Kinkennon with the Skull

Nothing more was ever learned of this case and it remained unsolved. The story might have ended way back in those dark depression days, except for a startling discovery many years later. Fast forward to October of 1976. A skull is found imbedded in sand and gravel near the riverbank on the Lyle Gleam farm, four miles southwest of Perry. The Dallas County Sheriff's Office was notified, and Deputy

Chapter Fifteen: Mystery Skull

Tom Kinkennon was assigned the task of digging into the case. Tom did his homework and uncovered the Danforth connection.

The skull, which was missing the lower jaw, was sent to State Archaeologist Dwayne Anderson of Iowa City. Anderson examined the skull and reported it had been in the river 20 to 30 years and belonged to a male who was between 17 and 35 years old when he died. Danforth was said to have been about 45 when he disappeared. Anderson said he has been told by Dr. Alton K Fisher of the University of Iowa, who also examined the skull, that the conclusions about age were tentative and that the man could have been older than 35. Anderson said the man who died entered the river near where the skull was found. If the skull had been carried for any great distance by the river's current, it would have been less well preserved and more eroded and scarred, he added. The Graney bridge was about a mile from the location on Lyle green's farm where the skull was found.

Several persons who remember the incident believe that one of the three men in the card game was killed by the other two and what Bert Bailey saw was the murderers dumping the body in the river. Kinkennon said he also assumes that the skull found was either Danforth's or that the farmhand was one of the two men throwing the bundle into the river. Harold Bailey, Bert's son and the brother of Leon, said that another man was reportedly sure it was a body they saw tossed off the bridge. Alta Storm, 74, who says her father, a close friend of Bert Bailey, was on the bridge watching the dragging operation the following morning and recalled Bert saying, "If that wasn't a body, I don't know what it was. In later years, Bert and my father would get together and talk about it. "He always said it was a body," she added.

Martell Pierce of Minburn said her father, James McCarthy, who was a deputy Sheriff and participated in the dragging operations, also believed Bailey's story about the body. She said a lot of strange things happened on that bridge and that the incident caused a lot of talk. "My father was sure it was a body that was thrown off the bridge, but they never did find it," she added.

Eva Snively and Mary Summy, widow and daughter of Elmer Snively, say they doubt Danforth would have left without saying goodbye unless something had happened to him or he was in trouble. Summy still has Danforth's prayer book and says he wouldn't have left it at our place if he'd still been alive. "I don't think he would have just run off. He intended to come back." Snively said. Her family has always thought that the body thrown off the bridge may have been Danforth.

"Every other body I know of that was lost in that area between 1926 and 1956 has been found," Kinkennon added. "We may never know for sure who's skull that is," he concedes. "But if we could find out who the other two guys in that card game were, we might be able to solve a 45-year-old murder."

So, that brings us to the present. Was a body thrown off the Graney Bridge and, if so, whose body was it? Sadly, as Former Deputy Tom Kinkennon noted, we may never know. I talked recently with Tom, who for several years has urged me to write this story. Tom had the skull, as well as all of his notes on the case. His law enforcement career took him to many places after leaving Dallas County. Somewhere along the way, all this material was lost. With modern DNA techniques, it's possible that William Danforth could have been ruled in or out as the victim. The town of Crosby, Indiana no longer exists, if it ever did. I have lots of reference material on Indiana ghost towns, but Crosby does not show up anywhere.

In 1931, the country was in the depths of depression. It was a time when gangsters, thugs, bootleggers and yeggs ran rampant over the countryside. Life was cheap. A drifter could disappear and be forever forgotten. The people he left back home, wherever that might have been, would simply assume he took up the transient life and was living in some hobo jungle along a railroad track to nowhere. Danforth, and the two other men that were involved in that fateful card game, may well have been such men.

Chapter Fifteen: Mystery Skull

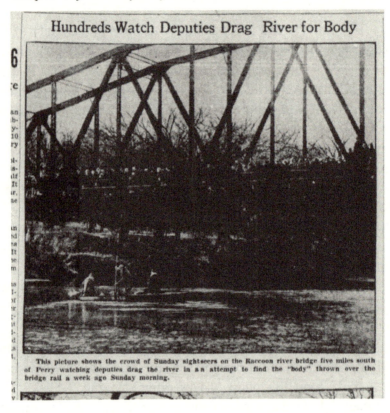

This picture shows the crowd of Sunday sightseers on the Raccoon river bridge five miles south of Perry watching deputies drag the river in an attempt to find the "body" thrown over the bridge rail a week ago Sunday morning.

Here's what I think. It was indeed a human body that was thrown off the Graney Bridge in the early morning hours of November 28, 1931. The body belonged to one of the other men in the card game, not William Danforth. It was a younger man, as the state archeologist reported. Danforth, after being involved in the murder, fled the area and continued his drifter ways, unknown and unnoticed. Sometime later, after he was sure he was not being pursued by the law, he returned to Indiana where he lived for many years. When he died, he took the secret of the Graney Bridge to the grave with him. This story would make a great novel. The title could be something like "Hard Times and the Raccoon's Tale." What do you think?

Chapter Sixteen

The Forty's and Fifty's

January 26, 1941...A Fight Over a Body

Here's a strange story about a colored coal miner. I was not able to find much information, other than a few newspaper accounts, but I am including it to show how real the divide between colored and white was, even in Dallas County, as recent as eighty years ago.

A murder took place in Zook Spur, an unplatted, unfiled, unincorporated mining village about three miles south of Madrid and just barely in Dallas County. According to Father Luigi Lugutti, a local priest, the town was also wholly "unattractive," as he described it in a 1928 letter. Largely owned by the Scandia Coal Company, the first residents came sometime around 1915. The town supported a store (owned by the coal company, of course), a doctor and several notorious drinking establishments. The post office was established in 1925. There was also a school where most of the boys only attended through the eighth grade, after-which they would go into the mines. This was common around the state through the 1930's. Many of the miners were European immigrants, with Italians making up the largest contingent. Most of these immigrants arrived before World War One, when immigration rules were less restrained and labor laws allowed long arduous hours. The village also had a close relationship with the railroad. It had its own depot and employed many of the colored men,

Chapter Sixteen: The Forty's and Fifty's

fresh from the railroad, as rookie miners. Robert Henderson, who murdered his wife in an argument, was probably one of those men. Here's what happened after the murder. The following are exact newspaper accounts:

Ruling Today in Burial Suit
Two Funeral Homes Vie Over a Body

Lengthy arguments before District Judge O. S. Franklin Monday failed to settle which of two funeral homes in Des Moines shall have possession of the body of a slain negro woman.

The arguments are to continue today, and the judge said he would decide immediately which funeral home shall have the body of Mrs Thelma Henderson, 46, who died last Friday at Perry Iowa, from gunshot wounds suffered at her home near Zook Spur, Iowa.

Robert Henderson, 61, her husband, is held without bond on a murder charge.

Property Right...The argument centered on whether there are any property rights in or to a dead body---whether a replevin action, used to obtain property, was properly used in the case.

Mrs. Henderson's body first was taken to the Estes Funeral Home here, on the order of relatives. The L. Fowler and Son Funeral Home obtained it from the Estes establishment under a replevin writ, claiming a written order from the husband that they prepare the body for burial.

The Estes home immediately asked that the writ of replevin be set aside, and the body be returned there, and the hearing Monday was on this motion.

Other States...W. Lawrence Oliver, Negro attorney for the Estes firm, cited several court cases from other states to back his contention that a body is not property in the eyes of the law, and that courts do not have the jurisdiction or power with which to issue a replevin writ for such a body. Charles Howard, Negro attorney for the Fowler firm, argued that all the cases cited showed that the next of kin, in this case the husband, have the right to order disposition of a body, and as Mrs. Henderson's body is held by the undertaker designated by her husband, nothing further need be done in the case.

Both agreed that they could find no Iowa court cases in which such a question was settled.
(Des Moines Register Tuesday December 30, 1941)

Fowler Wins Burial Ruling

The dispute between two Des Moines Negro funeral homes over possession of the body of a slain Negro woman was decided Tuesday in favor of the L Fowler and Son Funeral Home by District Judge O. S. Franklin.

The body is that of Mrs. Thelma Henderson, 46, who died last Friday from gunshot wounds suffered during a quarrel with her husband, Robert Henderson, 61, at their home near Zook Spur, Iowa.

Henderson, who is being held at Adel Iowa on a murder charge had given written consent to the Fowler establishment to take the body and prepare it for burial. The Dallas County coroner had sent the body to the Estes Funeral Home.

Judge Franklin held that the husband has the first right to determine disposition of his wife's body and overruled the contentions of attorneys for Estes that possession of a dead body could not lawfully be obtained under a replevin action.

In awarding the body to the Fowler establishment, Judge Franklin also carried out the written permission of

Chapter Sixteen: The Forty's and Fifty's

Henderson that the relatives of his wife select the coffin and place of burial.
(Des Moines Tribune…Thursday December 30, 1941)

Gets 35 Year Term

Robert Henderson, 61, Negro, of Zook Spur, Iowa, was sentenced to 35 years in the Iowa State Prison by District Judge W.S. Cooper. Henderson was convicted January 28 on a charge of shooting his wife Sylvia, December 6, 1941. She died December 20.
Mason City Globe Gazette…Thursday Feb. 5, 1942

Zook Spur Miner Appeals 35 Year Slaying Sentence

Des Moines---Robert Henderson, 61, Zook Spur, Iowa coal miner, has appealed to Iowa Supreme Court from a 35-year prison sentence was imposed February fourth at Adel, Iowa, in connection with the fatal shooting December 6 of his wife Sylvia. The case will be heard at the September term.
Carrol Daily Times Herold…Sat. March 14, 1942

Somehow, Mrs. Henderson's first name got changed from Thelma (in the first accounts) to Sylvia.

In November of 1942, the Iowa Supreme Court denied Henderson's appeal and confirmed the 35-year prison sentence. Considering his age at the time, it would probably be safe to conclude it was a life sentence.

Friday June 21, 1950…A Lucky Break

You would hardly believe this but it's true One of those "once in a lifetime events" happened twice to State Highway Patrolman Byron Hockenberry and to Dallas County Sheriff Evan Burger.

Hockenberry was driving along S.E. 14th Street at Railroad Ave at about 8:45 a.m. when he heard a state police radio report of an auto stolen in Adel. The license number of the stolen vehicle was 25-1076. Hockenberry looked at the license plate of the car just ahead of him. It was, that's right… you guessed it, 25-1076.

Hockenberry arrested the driver, Lodes Gorby, 16, who gave his address as Mount Pleasant, Michigan. The boy was taken to the Des Moines city jail.

About noon, Dallas County Sheriff Evan Burger came to Des Moines and took possession of the boy to return him to Adel. On the way back to Adel, Gorby told Burger that he and a "buddy" had left Michigan Sunday night in a car stolen from Gorby's father, Virgil Gorby. The boys drove to Des Moines where they spent a couple of days and then went on to Salt Lake City, he said. Returning to Des Moines Thursday night, they had a flat tire about two miles west of Adel. Gorby started walking to Adel to get a new tube for the tire. Passing the Conard Nash Company used car lot in Adel, Gorby decided to steal the Iowa car formerly owned by Doctor A.G. Felter of Van Meter and drive it to Des Moines.

A few minutes after this story was related to Sheriff Burger, the sheriff spotted an approaching car with a Michigan license. "That's my buddy," Gorby exclaimed. Naturally, the Sheriff made another arrest.

The second boy gave his name as Edward Busey Lowry, 18, also of Mount Pleasant. Lowry said that when Gorby did not return, he repaired the tire and started into Des Moines.

The boys spent a week cooling their heels in the Dallas County Jail. They were scheduled for release the following Saturday morning as Mr. Gorby, the man from whom they stole the car, was not going to press charges. However, an incident Friday night changed that for one of the boys. When Sheriff Burger walked into Edward Lowry's cell, the youth struck him on the head with a brush taken from a long-handled push broom. Sheriff Burger didn't take too kindly to this kind of treatment and filed charges of assault with intent to commit a felony

Chapter Sixteen: The Forty's and Fifty's

against Lowry, whose real identity was Edward Lower of Mount Pleasant MI.

August 31, 1950
Strikebound plant at Adel is dynamited.

About four p.m. on a warm Sunday afternoon in August, a loud blast shook the west end of Adel. Two men had attempted to blow up a clay planer at the United Brick and Tile plant. The blast of eight to ten sticks of dynamite did not damage the machine but blew a large hole in the floor of the pit. The reason for the fireworks was a labor dispute over wages and other issues. Plant employees, members of the C.I.O. Federation of Glass, Ceramics and Silica Sand Workers had been on strike about a month when the incident occurred.

Deputy Sheriff Ralph Grimm, Plant Manager L.E. (Pete) DeCamp, Ed parish, night watchman at the plant, and Bob Miller, office manager and assistant superintendent all rushed to the plant immediately after the explosion. As Grimm was driving on the road towards the clay pit, he saw two men walking in the opposite direction. The two men, Robert Seaboldt and Ivan Gowin, stopped at his car. Grimm asked Seaboldt what the two of them were doing in that area and Seaboldt replied, "We're just wondering around." This was about ten minutes after the explosion. Grimm advised them not to wonder too far away.

Grimm and the three other men followed two sets of footprints which led them to the scene of the explosion. Grimm said that the footprints stopped at the point of the explosion but began again on the other side and led to where Grimm had met Seaboldt and Gowin on the road leading out of the plant. The deputy Sheriff said he was able to follow the footprints because it had rained earlier in the day and the clay and mud were soft. He said that he took plaster casts of the footprints.

Grimm and the others checked the explosives house on the plant grounds and found that it was locked. He said the place where the explosives are kept is about 150 yards north of the scene of the explosion. "The dynamite used in the explosion appeared to have been laid on the side of the pit earlier," he added.

Plant Manager DeCamp found three unexploded sticks of dynamite and a short fuse in buckets on a bucket type elevator that lifts the clay from the pit. He said the explosion in the pit blew out an area of between 8 and 10 feet but did not damage the planer or elevator. DeCamp said that the explosion caused about $25 damage to platforms nearby.

Seaboldt and Gowin were arrested and charged with destruction of property by dynamite. They were escorted to the Dallas County jail where overnight accommodations were provided. The next day, they were released on $2500 bond each. Preliminary hearing was held on the following Thursday in Justice of the Peace H.L. Augustine's court. Bond was continued pending grand jury action during the September term of court.

The strike was settled before the trial began and the other, less destructive, workers returned to work. Trial was finally held on Wednesday November 8, 1950 in district court in Adel. Under cross examination by defense attorney John Connolly III of Des Moines, Deputy Grimm repeated his story. Grimm denied that he had taken a shoe from Seaboldt's home in Adel Sunday night when Seaboldt and Gowin were arrested. After several more questions on the subject of whether or not a shoe was taken from Seaboldt's apartment, County Attorney Don Shirley volunteered the information that a search warrant was obtained for Seaboldt's apartment on Monday but declined to say if anything had been taken from the apartment.

The two men plead guilty to a reduced charge of malicious mischief before Judge Earl Vincent. The judge tentatively set the date for sentencing to be November 22. The charge carries a penalty of a fine and a jail sentence not to exceed five years in the penitentiary.

The strike at the plant had begun on August 2. About 45 men were involved but only about 40 of them were members of the union. The workers struck over wages and other working conditions. The base

Chapter Sixteen: The Forty's and Fifty's

pay at the plant, at that time, was 80 cents an hour. The union was demanding a 30-cent hourly increase, along with vacation pay, a check off dues system, provisions for holidays and bonus plan. Negotiations between the union and plant, which was operated by the United Brick and Tile company of Kansas City Mo., broke off August 23rd. No work had been done at the plant since the strike began until the Saturday before the dynamiting when non-union supervisory employees began loading bricks onto trucks. The explosion was probably the result of the non-union employees working at the plant.

Attorney, John Connelly III, Bob Seaboldt and Ivan Gowin.

CRIME WAVE YET TO COME

Crime at its worst is yet to make its postwar return to Iowa.

The state bureau of criminal investigation, reporting this, crosses its long fingers and hopes the war lull will continue a long time.

No Bank Robberies.

There hasn't been a bank robbery in Iowa since before Pearl Harbor day. Murders of the sensational variety have been notably few.

Major case before the bureau as 1945 books are closed is the kidnaping Nov. 28 of State Highway Patrolman John Mahnke, 30, Denison, by two men and a woman he had started to question.

The kidnapers are believed to be Felix W. Kargol, Chicago, Ill., and Mr. and Mrs. Robert Lee Robertson, St. Louis, Mo. "Wanted" circulars have been sent to officers throughout the nation.

Increases.

R. W. (Doc) Nebergall, bureau chief, said the crime increase since VJ-day has been most marked in safe cracking, larceny, forgery, breaking and entering, and tire theft.

End of gasoline rationing was cited as the major factor in the postwar crime increase.

"It gives criminals a chance to go through the country without having to get stolen ration points," he said.

"Then there have been a lot of dislocations," he added. "It's a long trek home for many who had no money left."

The Des Moines Register Dec. 30, 1945

Chapter Sixteen: The Forty's and Fifty's
A Tavern Fight Turns Deadly

"Here lies Lester Moore, Four slugs from a .44, No Les No more."

That line can be found on a "Boothill" tombstone in one of my favorite tourist traps, Tombstone, Arizona. Here's the story of Lester Moore from the "Find a Grave" website*: In the late 1880s, Lester Moore worked as a Wells Fargo Station Agent in the Mexico-United States border town of Naco, Arizona. One day a man named Hank Dunstan arrived at the Wells Fargo station to pick up a package he was expecting. When Moore handed him a badly battered and mangled package, Dunstan became enraged over the condition of it and an argument ensued. The argument quickly became heated and both men reached for their guns. Moore was shot four times from Hank Dunstan's gun. Before Moore died, he managed to fire off one shot of his own, hitting Dunstan in the chest and Dunstan died from his injury. Lester Moore's body was transported to the nearby town of Tombstone, where he was buried in the Boothill Graveyard. There he became forever known for the epitaph inscribed on his headstone.*

It's a great story, however, there is no record of anyone named Lester Moore who was killed in Arizona Territory.

Dallas County, 1500 miles from Tombstone, has its own Lester Moore. The name may be spelled different, Mohr instead of Moore, but this story is true.

In Dallas County, the Lester Mohr dispute began in a Redfield tavern and was probably fueled by alcohol. Lester Mohr, 43, of Redfield, a soybean plant worker, and Robert Aldrich, 23, an Adel farmer, were engaged in a favorite tavern activity, drinking and arguing. After almost coming to blows in the tavern, the two were invited to take their fight elsewhere. They left the tavern and drove to a county road southeast of Redfield. There, they engaged in a fist fight that turned tragic.

The fight was witnessed by Jacqueline Davis, 16, former stepdaughter of Mohr, who lives with her grandparents near Redfield.

Kenneth Lenocker, 22, had been in the tavern when the disagreement began and also was present when the fight occurred. After the fight, in which Mohr received a severe blow to the abdomen, Aldrich drove Mohr home in Mohr's car. Jacqueline Davis drove Aldrich's car and was accompanied by Lenocker. Aldridge was quoted as saying that when he took Mohr home, he thought he was alright.

Mohr was found alive about 5 a.m. the next morning in an outbuilding at the home of Gordon Harding, where he boarded. Harding didn't realize Mohr had been badly injured. When George Hutchins, who also rented sleeping quarters from Harding, found him about 7 a.m., he was dead. An autopsy revealed that Mohr had died of internal bleeding caused by a severe blow to the abdomen.

Aldridge was tried in June but, after deliberating 23 hours, the jury could not reach an agreement. Judge Stanley E. Prall dismissed the jury and continued the case until the October term of court.

The retrial began on November 13. Court testimony revealed that Aldridge and Mohr had a fistfight May 2nd in Redfield after Mohr accompanied Jackie Davis, daughter of Mohr's former wife, to her home. Aldridge caused injuries to Mohr resulting in his death. In his instructions to the jury, the judge eliminated the charge of murder, telling the jurors they might find Aldrich guilty of manslaughter, assault with intent to do great bodily injury, or innocent.

On November 16, Aldrich was found guilty of assault with intent to commit great bodily injury in connection with the death of Lester Mohr. Under state law, Aldridge could have been sentenced to one year in either jail or the penitentiary or fined $500. District Judge George H. Sackett sentenced him to not more than one year at the Anamosa Men's Reformatory.

Chapter Sixteen: The Forty's and Fifty's
Saturday September 12, 1953...A Shaky Bandit

Every time I drive by the old former service station on Highway 169 on the south edge of Adel, I think of John Beane. Beane and my grandfather, Ollie Flinn, were good friends. Grandpa, a farmer, would always stop at Beane's "Cities Service" Station on his weekly trip to Adel. Whenever I was allowed to go along, I got to pick out some candy from the big white wood and glass enclosed display case next to the cash register. This was in the late 40's and 50's. Remembering that time is why I found this story especially interesting. The crime was more amusing than dangerous.

Bandit Loses Nerve, Gives Gun to Victim is how the headline in the Des Moines Register appeared. Bean, 55, had just finished putting 15 gallons of gasoline into a car when the driver pulled a gun on him and said, "This is a holdup." The man then told Bean to go to the washroom and locked him in, or so he thought. But Bean left the washroom by a rear door and jotted down the car's license number, then returned to the washroom just in time to be let out of the front door. Surprised to be freed by the very man who had just locked him up, Beane stepped out as the bandit handed him the gun with which he had robbed him. The shaky bandit said, "I just don't have nerve enough left to do this." He then added, "Take this gun to pay for the gas." The bandit also returned $28.50 he had scooped into his pockets. He then left.

The gunman was arrested about 20 minutes later, near Winterset, by Madison County Sheriff Cecil Lance. He was identified as Floyd E. McGee, 33, of Sioux Falls S.D., a former marine. McGee was returned to Dallas County Sheriff Evan Burger and became a guest in the Dallas County Jail that night.

McGee told Bean, after the incident, that he couldn't have shot him even if he had resisted. "The gun was a rim-fire pistol but contained center-fire cartridges," he explained.
Not convinced, Bean pulled the trigger a couple times on the loaded gun. The gun wouldn't fire.

Asked why he had done it, McGee said he was broke and out of work.

State Motor Vehicle Authorities said that McGee was driving a car reported stolen Friday night from C.J. Carlson of West Des Moines. Carlson, a former highway patrolman, operated a locker plant. Carlson's car was stolen from the alley in back of the West Des Moines police station. West Des Moines police also found an abandoned 1940 Buick, owner unknown, with a single license plate on it. This car is believed to be the one McGee drove into Des Moines Friday night. The license plate was one that Hi Schmidt of Lake Park had reported lost or stolen September 6th at Spirit Lake.

McGee said he would take the car back that he had just stolen in Des Moines and try to find some work. That plan would have to be postponed for a while, however. Dallas County Sheriff Evan Burger charged McGee with carrying a concealed weapon and going armed with intent to commit robbery. McGee pleaded guilty to both charges and was sentenced to two terms of five years each in the State Penitentiary in Fort Madison. That seems a bit harsh for no more harm than was done. Hopefully, he received an early parole. Grandpa and John Beane would not have wanted him to waste away in prison like that.

Sept. 9, 1954...Brotherly Love

The badly decomposed body of John Bodenberger, a farmer of about 60-years of age, was found in a patch of weeds by the Raccoon River just south of the old Graney bridge near Perry. Leo Bodenberger, brother of the dead man, had led officers to the place where the body was found. John Bodenberger had lived alone in a one room home near where his body was discovered.

Before leading the officers to the body, Leo Bodenberger had been arrested at a Des Moines hotel, by Sheriff Evan Berger, after a check, purportedly signed by John Bodenberger, had been cashed at a Des Moines surplus store. A search of the hotel room disclosed John

Chapter Sixteen: The Forty's and Fifty's

Bodenberger's American Legion membership card and checkbook. The checkbook was found in a shoe. Burger said Leo Bodenberger had given officers a statement saying his brother had been shot with a 12-gauge shotgun on August 30th. There was a rope around the neck of the body when it was discovered, the Sheriff said.

An autopsy on the badly decomposed body showed death was caused by a blow to the head. A broken gun stock and spent shotgun shells were found by the body. The shotgun, that Leo fired at his brother John, apparently did not kill him so Leo beat his brother over the head twice with it and then tied a rope around his neck to drag his body to the weeds before taking his things.

Leo pleaded guilty to murder, so there was no jury trial. A sentencing hearing was set for Oct. 6, 1954. At the hearing, Bodenberger's attorney, George Soumas, reviewed the evidence, starting with the two statements by Leo that showed premeditation. Bodenberger admitted he took the gun to the riverbank and used it for the murder weapon. He also admitted to coming back for it the next day. Soumas pointed out that Bodenberger never denied any of the evidence and he repeatedly declined to testify in his own defense.

Sheriff Burger told Dallas County Court Judge George Sackett, "I believe Leo has told me the truth to the best of his ability." The sheriff urged lenience. "I think that this is one place where the scales of mercy should be tipped to the side of Leo, and it is my recommendation that the court see fit not to impose the death penalty."

Robert Frush, Leo's court-appointed defense attorney, also recommended his life be spared and begged the court for leniency.

Bodenberger was calm at his sentencing, standing before the judge with his hands in his pockets and eyes cast down. The judge explained that it might have been different if he had testified in his own behalf. He then pronounced sentence of imprisonment in Fort Madison for the rest of his life. Bodenberger seemed resigned and grateful that the ordeal was over.

Leo Bodenberger died in Fort Madison Prison in January 1972.

Chapter Seventeen

Minburn Bank Robbery

The Dallas County Savings Bank of Minburn was organized in 1914. It's president, in 1951, was N. P. Black of Des Moines, who was also state Superintendent of banking. Scott Ellis, a prominent Dallas County farmer, was vice president. In all it's 37 years of existence, it had never been robbed. On the afternoon of Tuesday May 1, 1951, that was about to change.

It was around 3:20 in the afternoon. Cashier W. Lester Crumley, 55, was busy preparing to close when a man of about 30 years of age, wearing a light blue work jacket and trousers, appeared suddenly at the back window of the cashier's cage. "Don't you ever lock that door over there?" the man asked, pointing to the front door. Crumley told him they were just about to close. With that, the man went back to the door, shut it with a shove and then walked back over to Crumley. He was carrying a sawed-off 12-gauge shotgun. Holding up a sack, he ordered, "Fill it with money!"

"He was new to me," Crumley admitted. "I'd never seen him before. He was jumpy and nervous all the time he was in the bank. As he talked, I smelled liquor on his breath."

The cashier didn't hesitate. He knew it was a hold up and told the others working with him, Miss Marsha Luellen and Miss Marjorie Briggs, what was happening. Reaching down into the drawer where the counter cash was kept, he put about $1000, maybe $1500, into the paper bag. As he handed it back, the robber said in a rough voice, "You've got more than that around here. Give me more than that."

When Crumley started for the vault, the robber ordered him to stop. He then asked, "Can I get around there with you inside the cage?"

"He was still holding that gun on me, so I let him through a door on the south side of the cage, up in front," Crumley explained. "I had to open the safe by using the combination. I was worried I might not get the safe open the first time and I wondered what he might do if I failed. He was pretty jittery through all of this. More so than we in the bank were."

The vault door did open right away and Crumley went to the small safe the bank kept in there and got some more money. "I put it into the sack, and he said something about that's better. Then he ordered the girls into the vault with me and tried to close the vault door. He had some trouble, but finally got the job done. He shoved the bolts into place and there we were, locked up."

Apparently, the bandit left hurriedly through the front door and drove away in the car he had parked at the curb just outside. In his flight, he left his gun just inside the front entrance of the bank, where it was found a short time later.

"From inside the vault," Crumley added, "we could hear noises in the bank. At first, we thought it might be the robber, but then we guessed it might be a customer. We called and a man came back to the safety deposit section door at the rear of the vault. By luck, this rear door was wide open and only a heavy wire screen held us inside. The man was Phil Messamer. who lives between Minburn and Adel. We told him what had happened and asked him to get somebody to cut the screen."

Murder and Mayhem in Dallas County

Marcia Luellen, Marjorie Briggs and W. Lester Crumley in front of the vault

Messamer went next door to the Raney Garage and Lew Raney, the operator, summoned a mechanic, Darrell Cornelison. Cornelison succeeded in cutting away the screen. He made a hole in the screen about three-foot-high and three-foot-wide so Crumley, Miss Briggs and Miss Luellen could crawl out and get back into the bank itself. The vault is about 15 feet long and 12 feet wide with the heavy mesh screen

Chapter Seventeen: Minburn Bank Robbery

separating the safety deposit box section from the main vault space. It has two doors, the front one leading from the cashier's cage and the rear one opening into the bank's office near the back of the building.

Crumley said the women held up under the strain very well. Cornelison, however, declared "they were pretty white in the face when I reached them and set them free."

The cashier immediately telephoned Dallas County Sheriff Evan Burger at Adel to report the holdup. Burger sent out a general alarm and roadblocks were set up promptly in the area.

Iowa Bureau of Criminal Investigation agents and Iowa agents for the Federal Bureau of Investigation, (FBI) joined Sheriff Burger in a full investigation of the robbery. Fingerprints were taken in various places in the bank. Tire marks in front of the bank were also taken in cast form.

The bandit was further identified as about six feet tall and weighing between 165 and 170 pounds. He was described as slender but well built. He wore no mask and was said to have been clean-shaven. He wore a billed cap pushed back on his head when he entered the bank. He appeared to have blonde hair, parted in the middle.

Crowds of townspeople, and a number of farmers who were in town, gathered around the front of the one-story brick bank building while officers conducted their investigation. The bank was about a block from the main highway. A grocery store was on the north side and the Raney Garage was on the south.

After the excitement was over, Cashier Crumley said he remembered, when he first saw the bandit's shotgun, that the bank had an old revolver inside the vault. "I thought once or twice of trying to get it," he said "But then I recalled that it hadn't been fired for several years, at least, and I decided against taking a chance on having a gun battle. I just let it lie there in the vault."

More than two hours after the robbery, authorities received a report that a car, answering the description of the auto used in the holdup, had been pulled out of the mud on a side road south of Minburn. Sheriff Burger was told that the driver of the car, a green Dodge sedan, offered $20 to a farmer to pull it to the paved highway. It was reported that the man then headed south on Highway 169. That road intersects with Highway 64 only five miles South of Minburn. The driver could have gone east, west or south from that four-way corner.

About $1500 of the loot was in $1 bills. There were several packages of $5, $10 and $20 bills and perhaps a few $100 bills. The banks money was insured under the Federal Deposit Insurance Corporation. It was later established the stolen loot amounted to $11,629.

Crumley had joined the bank staff in 1927 as cashier. Miss Briggs, 18, who resided on a farm near Minburn, had become a bookkeeper in the bank only a few weeks earlier. Miss Luellen, 54, had been with the bank since 1916, first as bookkeeper and more recently as assistant cashier.

The hold up here was Iowa's first armed daylight bank robbery since August 2nd, 1950, when a man held up the Bronson Iowa office of a Sioux City bank and fled with $870. That man tied up the bank manager, waited on two customers and then fled. He had not been arrested at that time.

The search for the robber soon swung to the south as authorities followed a strong lead that he was headed toward Kansas City, Mo. It was almost definitely established that the armed bandit was in Des Moines within two hours after the 3:20 p.m. holdup. Further questioning of patrons had strengthened the theory that the tall slender bandit was at the Barrelhouse Tavern at Beaver and Douglas Avenues between five and six p.m. Tuesday. During that time, the man believed to be the robber cashed two $100 bills in buying drinks for the house. He got back about $180 in change. Bank officials said there were fifteen $100 bills in the bank loot. While in the tavern, the man remarked that he was headed for Kansas City, Mo. The bartender, J. Bradford, and several other patrons, said he was half drunk at the time.

Dallas County Sheriff Evan Burger said that new evidence had convinced him that the bandit was the man who was stuck in the mud in a side road off Hwy 169, about four miles south of Minburn, shortly

Chapter Seventeen: Minburn Bank Robbery

after the holdup. That man was pulled out of the mud by a farmer, Francis Friesz, who had no knowledge of the hold up at the time. Burger said that a handful of Federal Brand 12-gauge shotgun shells had been found near the spot where the car was stuck. The unfired shells were the same brand as the one found in the Chamber of the sawed-off shotgun used in the holdup. That shotgun, left just inside the bank entrance, was studied in the laboratories of the Iowa Bureau of criminal investigation.

The bandit was described as about 30 years old, about six feet tall and weighing about 168 pounds, gray eyes, ruddy complexion and wearing blueish work clothes. He was believed to be driving a 1949 or 1950 green Dodge or Chrysler.

By Friday of that same week, the bandit was captured. Edward Emil Weise, formerly of Elbow Lake, Minnesota, was arrested in Erie, Kansas. Neosha County Sheriff Ernest Craig, alerted by the Federal Bureau of investigation on a lead the FBI established in Des Moines, arrested Wiese in an Erie Tavern about 5 p.m. Thursday May 3. He said Wiese had signed a sworn statement admitting the robbery. Wiese had $8634.43 in two briefcases when arrested. Wiese said the $11,629 dollar holdup was a spur-of-the-moment job. "It was my first robbery attempt," he admitted.

No detailed account was given of the nearly $3000 missing from the bank loot. Sheriff Craig, however, said Wiese told of spending money freely along his escape route from Iowa to Erie. Erie is about 150 miles south of Kansas City Mo. and nearly 400 miles south of Des Moines. James Dalton, FBI special agent in charge of the Omaha, Nebraska Division, said that Wiese would be returned to Des Moines to face a federal charge.

The charge filed in US District Court in Des Moines was for bank robbery by force and violence and by putting fear into bank employees by use of a dangerous weapon.

Wiese confirmed earlier reports of his whereabouts. He was the man stuck in the mud about four miles south of Minburn shortly after the holdup. Wiese had received a lucky break by getting stuck on the seldom used side road south of Minburn. That side road acted as a perfect temporary hideout for the robber.

He did stop at the Barrel House Tavern in Des Moines between 5 and 6 p.m. the day of the robbery, as authorities had believed. While there, he produced two $100 bills in buying drinks for the house. It was during his Tavern visit that Wiese made remarks that led to his capture. He told patrons he was going to Kansas City, Missouri and also was going to visit a sister in Erie, Kansas. As a result of that tip, Sheriff Craig in Erie was alerted by the FBI for possible appearance of the Minburn bandit.

Wiese, a 26-year-old former farmhand, had worked on two farms near Pocahontas, Iowa in the last two years under the name of Robert Smith. He told of driving to St. Joseph Missouri from Des Moines and then continuing on to Erie. Wiese said he came to Erie to visit a girl he had met during a visit last Easter.

Wiese was arrested within 15 minutes of arriving in Erie. He was spotted driving a 1950 cream colored Dodge bearing Iowa license 74-4362. Earlier, it had been reported the bandit was driving a green Dodge with Iowa license plates. The car had been stolen from a salesman in Bemidji, Minnesota, which is near Wiese' hometown of Elbow Lake. Wiese admitted stealing the car after his own auto, a 1941 Mercury, had broken down at Bemidji about ten days prior. He had transferred license plates from his car to the stolen auto. Wiese had flashed a lot of money in the Tavern where he was captured.

Wiese claimed he never planned to commit the robbery and that he didn't remember much about it. He told authorities he was drunk at the time. Crumley, the bank cashier, said he smelled liquor on the bandit's breath and Friesz, the farmer who pulled him out from the mud, said he appeared to have been drinking.

Chapter Seventeen: Minburn Bank Robbery

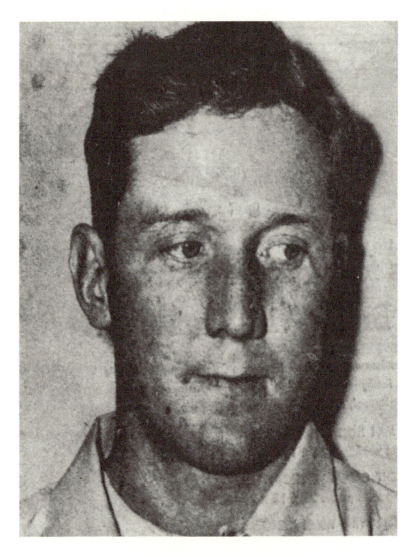

Edward Emil Weise

Murder and Mayhem in Dallas County

Wiese had no previous criminal record but had been sought in Iowa on two bad check charges. The previous March 19, Wiese, who had been working on the farm of Mr. and Mrs. William Spaniard, was accused of forging $300 worth of checks against the Spaniard's bank account in Pocahontas, Iowa. Another bad check charge was later brought against Wiese in Corning, Iowa. Wiese, who had left the Spaniard farm on March 17th, was reported seen April 8th South of Bedford, Iowa. No other word came from him until his arrest in Erie, Kansas.

Weise waived preliminary hearing and agreed to return to Iowa to face federal charges in connection with the bank robbery. He was arraigned before US commissioner Sam Terbovitch, who set bond at $5000 and committed him to the Wyandotte County Jail in Kansas City, Kansas to await return to Iowa. Of the $11,629 dollars stolen, authorities recovered all but $1,469 from hiding places in the car. Weise spent the missing money on liquor and a new outfit of clothing he bought at Brookfield, Missouri. Considering the amount of money, almost $15,000 today, Weise was either a spiffy dresser or a heavy drinker (or both).

The young bandit was brought back to Iowa and housed in the Polk County Jail. He was accommodated in Polk County, rather than Dallas, as bank robbery was a federal crime instead of a state crime.

The charge carried a maximum sentence of 25 years in the penitentiary. A state charge of bank robbery carried a penalty of from ten years to life imprisonment. Under the Iowa indeterminate sentence law, this had made a life term mandatory in the past, but the 1951 legislature had amended the law to give judges discretion in making sentence. A life term would be mandatory for prisoners received at penitentiaries before the effective date of the act, July 4th. After that, the term would be as decided by the judge, the minimum being ten years. Wiese' best hope, therefore, was that he remained under federal and not state charges, but if he was sentenced under state charges, it had better be after the Fourth of July and by a lenient judge.

Chapter Seventeen: Minburn Bank Robbery

Doctor A.S. Price was named by Federal Judge William C Riley to determine the mental competency of Wiese. Lehan T. Ryan, court appointed attorney for Wiese, asked that such an examination be made when Wiese appeared before Riley. Wiese' arrangement was delayed until after results of Doctor Prices examination were known.

Meantime, the prisoner received visitors at his new abode. His parents, Mr. and Mrs. Emil Wiese, gray haired farm folk from Minnesota, saw their son for the first time in more than a year. When they visited him at the Polk County jail, Wiese confessed that he had made a terrible mistake in staging a one-man holdup of the bank. The Wiese's had not heard from their son since he left a farm job in Minnesota in February 1950, until he was arrested for the Iowa robbery. The father was 68, and the mother 59. They were accompanied by two of Edward's sisters, Mrs. Knute Westrom and Mrs. Norman Westrom, and a brother-in-law, Mr. Norman Westrom. They declined to discuss their visit or their plans except to say that they would return to Minnesota the following Tuesday.

Mrs. Weise said Edward had never been the same since he came home from World War Two. He served from 1944 to 1946 and was with occupation forces in Japan briefly. Mr. and Mrs. Wiese have six other children.

Since Wiese had pleaded guilty, a trial was avoided. Judge Riley held a sentencing hearing on June 15, 1951. In asking for leniency, Lehan T Ryan, his court appointed counsel, told the court that Wiese, last January, started going to Pocahontas taverns. His drinking was the only amusement he knew. He started following that amusement, Ryan said. "And that, I think, is what eventually led him into trouble."

Ryan, reading a written statement to the court, said Wiese told him he remembers entering the bank and after he got inside the door, the thought flashed in his mind as to what he was doing there and he sort of half turned around to leave. "Someone in the bank then apparently spoke to him," Ryan continued "and he said from then on his mind is a blank and that about all he knew of his actions in the bank, or what had been told to him since, he had read in the papers."

Judge Riley told Wiese, "Investigation revealed that you have a splendid family of hardworking industrious religious people. But," the judge continued "I can't believe what you say about not knowing what you did." The judge cited several acts which he said all indicated premeditation. All these acts, the judge explained, makes the crime more aggravated.

Assistant District Attorney Cloid I. Level related the events of Wiese's life from his leaving his farm home near Elbow Lake Minnesota, in the fall of 1949, until his arrest. Wiese admitted taking a cream-colored car at Bemidji, Minnesota and using it in the robbery about 10 days later. Wiese's own car, bought while he was working at Pocahontas, had broken down. The assistant prosecutor said also that Albia, Iowa authorities had reported a hotel clerk had identified Wiese as the man who held him up and took $65 in the hotel last April 15th. He said Wiese has denied that. Judge Riley said he was not attaching any significance to the Albia identification, but he queried Wiese about the shotgun which he had sawed off both at barrel and butt before robbing the bank. Wiese said he bought the gun last fall for pheasant hunting. "Where did you get the gun?" the judge asked concerning the day of the robbery.

"I had it in the car," Wiese replied. He had moved it from his own to the other car when he stole it. The judge asked Wiese when he had sawed off the gun. He indicated he did that in the morning or early afternoon of the day he held up the bank. He later left it loaded at the bank's entrance.

Concerning the car theft, the judge commented that, "Wiese's changing of the license plates indicated you thought things through pretty well. Each one of these things was a more aggravated step," the judge continued. "I can't believe what you say about not knowing what you did."

Edward Emil Wiese was sentenced to 15 years in a federal penitentiary for the hold up. Judge Riley said the sentence imposed on

Chapter Seventeen: Minburn Bank Robbery

Wiese would have been 25 years had it not been for his youth and for his confession of the robbery.

Wiese showed little emotion as the judge pronounced sentence. The prisoner appeared relieved as a deputy U.S. Marshall led him from the courthouse courtroom. As he left, Wiese turned to Ryan, his court-appointed attorney, and said, "Thanks a lot."

Chapter Eighteen

Murder Among the Tropical Fish

The scream probably could have been heard by anyone within two miles of the scene. When Mrs. Robert King entered the isolated business site at around 10 a.m. Tuesday March 9, 1965, she found a gruesome sight. Her business partner and close friend, Mrs. Myrtle Cumpston, lay dead on the floor with a 45-caliber bullet in the back of her head.

C & K Aqualand, a tropical fish aquarium business located in rural Dallas County near Redfield, was co-owned by Mrs. Cumpston and Mrs. King. The two women and their husbands had met 10 years earlier through a mutual interest in tropical fish. They first operated the company together out of the King home in West Des Moines. Because the business grew so rapidly, they moved it to a building on the Cumpston farm, located on an unpaved road a quarter-of-a-mile east of Redfield, where the Cumpstons had lived for 30 years. The Kings built a house a half-mile from the Cumpston residence in 1961. The day-to-day operation was conducted by the two women.

After finding the body of her partner, Mrs. King telephoned her husband, who was an engineer for WHO Radio and Television in Des Moines. Robert King, as luck would have it, had the day off and was working around their home 1/2 mile north of the Cumpston home. King

Chapter Eighteen: Murder Among the Tropical Fish

called Dr. Keith Chapler of Dexter, the Cumpston's private physician, and also Dallas County Medical Examiner. At Dr. Chapler's direction, King then called Dallas County Sheriff John T. Wright.

Sheriff Wright sought aid from the Iowa Bureau of Criminal Investigation in Des Moines. Gifford Strand, special agent for the Bureau, was sent to the scene. Strand quickly speculated that the motive was robbery. A cash box, estimated to contain about $50, was missing from the shop. Friends and neighbors of the Cumpstons could think of no enemies of the dead woman or other reason for the murder.

Dr. Chapler ordered an autopsy which determined that death was due to a gunshot wound in the back of the head, causing extensive brain damage. The single shot was fired as she leaned over to get a ceramic figurine out of a display case and it occurred between 8 and 10 a.m. that morning.

No tire tracks could be found in the snow that would give the authorities any clues. All lights in the building housing the aquarium were on. The aquarium building was located about 90 feet from the Cumpston home.

The 80-acre Cumpston farm, located on an unpaved road that stretched from Highway 90 to Highway 6, was just east of Redfield. Since 1953, Charles Cumpston had been a livestock inspector for the animal disease eradication division of the US Department of Agriculture. Formerly, he had operated a poultry and hatchery business in Adel. He had lived on the farm about 30 years.

Charles Cumpston had left home that morning about 8 a.m. to drive to Oskaloosa to inspect some animals in that area. He had checked into a motel there, thinking he would be away from home overnight. He was soon located at the motel and told to return home immediately.

King said he and his wife became acquainted with the Cumpstons about ten years earlier through membership in a tropical fish club. Four years prior, the two families went into business together with their shop and office in the basement of the King's home in West Des Moines. King said the business outgrew the West Des Moines house, so he and his wife bought ten acres of land from the Cumpstons and built a new home. They had just moved into it a few months earlier.

The two women did most of the work at the shop, opening up at 10 a.m. each day. The shop served some retail customers, but mostly sold wholesale to city retail shops that stock tropical fish. The two families also did some breeding of fish, mostly guppies. They stocked about 50 varieties of tropical fish.

Because the in-home business was located in such a remote area, the murderer may have been familiar with the operation. He might also have known the general banking habits of the owners. The shop did its heaviest trade on weekends. On Monday of that week, Mrs. Cumpston and Mrs. King had driven to Des Moines to deposit nearly $700.00 from the weekend business. The shop was closed on Monday's.

The case of Myrtle Zelda Cumpston remains, to this day, unsolved. It is listed on the Iowa Cold Case website with the following information:

> Homicide
> Myrtle Zelda (Dickerson) Cumpston
> 60 YOA
> C & K Aqualand
> Redfield, IA
> Dallas County
> DCI Case # 65-00401
> March 9, 1965

When the Iowa Division of Criminal Investigation (DCI) established the Cold Case Unit in 2009, Myrtle Cumpston's murder was one of approximately 150 cases listed on the Cold Case Unit's new website as those the DCI hoped to solve using the latest advancements in DNA technology.

Although federal grant funding for the DCI Cold Case Unit was exhausted in December 2011, the DCI continues to assign agents to investigate cold cases as new leads develop or as technological

Chapter Eighteen: Murder Among the Tropical Fish

advances allow for additional forensic testing of original evidence. Who knows? Maybe someday we will know who committed this murder "among the tropical fish."

Mrs. Myrtle Cumpston

Chapter Nineteen

The Try-Angle Inn Murder

The afternoon of July 30, 1974 was a typical summer day in Iowa, hot and humid. It was a Tuesday and hay baling was in full swing on many of the surrounding farms. Teen-age farm boys, shirtless and sweaty, were tossing bales onto hay racks in the fields or stacking bales in hot dusty barns. Elsewhere, whole families were walking beans or tending livestock. It was not a scene where you would expect to find a cowardly and cold-blooded murder, but that's just what happened.

The Try-Angle Inn sat two-and-a-half miles west of Adel along Highway 6. It was on a triangle shaped piece of ground, formed by the Adams/Colfax township line on the south and Highway 6 angling slightly from north to south and intersecting with County P58 on the west. The Conoco gas station included a concrete block building approx. 30 ft. square where tires were fixed, automobiles were greased and serviced, and even farm equipment was sometimes repaired. A small cluttered office building was attached to the west wall. The Try-Angle Inn and restaurant served an important purpose for this farming area.

The restaurant building was a few feet from the east wall of the block building and sat at a slight angle to it. On another corner of the lot sat a modern two-bedroom house that the proprietors, Dick and

Chapter Nineteen: The Try-Angle Inn Murder

Lucy Yager, called home. People had long since stopped questioning why it was "Try-Angle" and not "Triangle," and just accepted the name.

Try-Angle Inn Service Station and Restaurant

Dick and Lucy had owned and operated the business since 1947. They purchased it after the death of Dick's father, who had started the business in 1933. It was a busy truck stop along Highway 6 in its early days when that road carried much of the nation's traffic. After the opening of Interstate 80 in the early 60's, and loss of most of the truck traffic, The Try Angle catered more to the farming community and local commuters.

I grew up on a farm in the neighborhood that it served and have many memories of the place. It was where my father and grandfather would take tractor and implement tires to be repaired. Sometimes I got to tag along. One of my fondest memories was of Grandpa carefully counting out a nickel and a penny from his bib overalls pocket so I could buy an eight oz. Coke or a Grapette soda from the cooler located in the station office.

Dick and Lucy Yager were honest and hard-working people. They were also very friendly and well-liked by everyone who knew them. They worked six days a week and seldom took vacations. Dick ran the station, servicing cars and trucks and repairing tires when not pumping gas. He seldom turned down any tire repair and would even wrestle the big tractor rears that farmers brought to him in the back of their pickups.

The restaurant, featuring "Home Cooked Meals," was operated by Lucy Yager. She was the cook/chef and the kitchen was her domain. Waitresses were farm wives and daughters, hired from the neighborhood. They were not paid a whole lot but were always treated well. Breakfast and dinner (the noon meal was dinner) were the only meals served. Breakfast consisted of two choices: eggs (any style you wanted) and pancakes. Of course, there was always lots of hot coffee. The dinner menu consisted of one entrée. It varied from day to day and season to season but always consisted of meat, potatoes and a vegetable. Pie was included. There was usually a choice of three double crusted fruit pies and maybe a custard. Tea or coffee was also included, but if you wanted a soda pop, you had to pay extra for it. Hamburgers were available at all times for the "youngsters," but adults usually ordered the "Noon Special."

The restaurant also filled a need in this rural area. The decades following WW II saw big changes in the lives of farm families. Women had earned their right to be in the workplace during the war when they stepped up and replaced the men who were needed overseas. They did not all go back to the domestic life after the war. By the fifty's and sixty's, many a farm wife had joined this "working wife" revolution and had taken jobs outside the home to supplement the meager farm incomes of the time.

The decades after the war also saw major changes in farming methods. Large modern machinery allowed one man to do what had

Chapter Nineteen: The Try-Angle Inn Murder

required several before. The threshing crew was a thing of the past, but there were still jobs that required a "crew" or, at least, a few extra hands for the day. Ear corn was still shelled in a day-long operation. Hay baling meant extra help for a day or two. With the wife working in town, the farmer needed a way to feed this extra help. If you didn't fill the stomach at noon, you could not expect an efficient work crew in the afternoon. That's where the Try-Angle-Inn Restaurant came in. You only needed to tell Lucy, in the morning, how many would be in your party, and dinner and a table would be waiting at noon. Many of these "bachelor by day" farmers ate breakfast there and made arrangements with Lucy for feeding their help before leaving. Word of the noon special at the Triangle always found its way around the neighborhood before noon time.

The restaurant operated from a cash box, but Dick ran the gas station out of his back pocket. He did not have a cash register at the station and always carried a big wad of bills in his wallet.

It was mid-afternoon on that Tuesday. The dinner rush was over, the tables were cleaned, and the dishes washed. There were only four customers in the restaurant, Thomas Grady and Gene Lindstrom and their wives. Thomas and Gene were dump truck operators from Otho, Iowa (near Fort Dodge) and had been hauling rock from Redfield to Sigourney. They had been customers of the Try-Angle Inn for several years. Thomas said he considered Dick "one of the friendliest men I ever met." On this day, they had met their wives there, and were planning to go on to Des Moines that evening to spend the night. Their wives had driven down from Otho in Grady's pickup.

Dick Yager seldom stopped working but he had taken the time to briefly visit with the Gradys and Lindstroms before returning to a tire repair in his service building. None of them paid much attention to the dark blue older pickup pulling onto the drive.

Robert Lewis Smith, 39, and Ivyle Kimmel, 30, both unemployed and from the Warren County town of St. Mary, had been drinking most of the day. They were looking over places to burglarize and had decided to avoid Adel, as it was a county seat town with a sheriff's office.

The facts of what happened next were later admitted to by Smith. Smith got out of the truck and inquired as to the location of the men's toilet. Yager told him it was in the rear of the building and Smith left. He later went back to Kimmel's pickup and took a revolver from the glove compartment. He then reentered the gas station carrying the weapon in a raised position.

The four customers and Lucy Yager all heard a loud bang. Grady thought a tire blew up and he ran outside and towards the service building. He saw Smith run from the building towards Kimmel's pickup. When Grady got to the station door, Smith briefly pointed the gun at him.

After realizing that the noise was a gunshot, Lindstrom pushed the three women to the floor and also ran out towards the station. Smith pointed the gun at him, also, but never fired at either man. The pickup then sped away from the scene.

Dick Yager staggered about 15 ft. to the restaurant door and collapsed. He had been shot in the chest just below his heart. Lucy said she heard him shout for help. (Others later claimed they heard him say "I didn't know them."

As the suspects headed east on Highway 6 towards Adel, Grady ran to his dump truck where he had left his suitcase. He always carried a .38-caliber pistol when he worked out of town and he quickly retrieved it. Grady, armed with the 38, then jumped in his pickup and gave chase. On the outskirts of Adel, the suspects turned south on what they thought was a county road. It actually was a farm lane leading to the Van Fossen farm, and a dead end after that. Grady turned on the road and, seeing the blue pickup turning around, pulled his pickup across the road in an attempt to block their getaway. He then hid behind his pickup, gun in hand. The blue pickup headed right for him as two shots were fired from the passenger side. Fortunately, the shots missed their mark. When Grady returned fire, he was sure he struck the blue pickup at least twice. (It was later determined that he had struck the

Chapter Nineteen: The Try-Angle Inn Murder

pickup in the passenger door and tailgate but had not hit either passenger). The suspects swerved, just before hitting Grady's pickup and made their getaway by driving through the shallow ditch and back to Highway 6. They then proceeded east through Adel and turned south on Highway 169, tossing the gun in the ditch somewhere along the way (the gun was never found). Grady had emptied his gun in the Van Fossen Lane shootout and, not having any more ammo, gave up the chase and went to the police station to report the shooting.

Dick Yager was rushed by ambulance to Iowa Methodist Hospital in Des Moines where he was pronounced dead. It was determined that he had been struck by a 22-caliber bullet and the shot was fired from a distance of eight to ten inches. Robbery was thought to be the motive, as Yager's casual handling of money was well known. However, his wallet had not been touched.

Dallas County Sheriff John Wright and his deputies worked on the case without let-up. The Iowa Bureau of Criminal Investigation, and the Warren, Clarke, Polk and Madison County Sheriff's Offices, also worked on the case. By Thursday morning they had located the suspects in a farmhouse near St. Mary in Warren County. Warren County Sheriff William Mathews said the men had "guns around them" but did not resist arrest. A dark blue older pickup, found at the farmhouse, was sent to the state crime lab for investigation. The two men were returned to Dallas County and held on $100,000 bond each.

Trial was held in Dallas County the following March (1975) in the court of Judge Van Wifvat. Both men were found guilty. Ivyle Kimmel was sentenced to 50 years in prison for second degree murder. Robert L. Smith also was found guilty of second-degree murder and received a life sentence.

Murder and Mayhem in Dallas County

Ivyl Kimmel and Robert Smith (wearing sunglasses) being escorted by Deputy Sheriff Robert DeCamp

Smith appealed his sentence to the Iowa Supreme Court. I have read a synopsis of the appeal. It is full of "legaleeze" and lawyer talk. However, the testimony put forth by Smith, in seeking to reduce his sentence, is quite interesting. Here is his story and I'll let you decide its merit:

Smith admitted to firing the fatal shot but took the position that it was an accident. In essence, Smith maintained (1) the gun was carried by him into the gas station for the sole purpose of attempting to sell it to Mr. Yager; (2) he did not realize it might be loaded until entry into the station; (3) the weapon was then raised only to check the cylinder for bullets and he slightly pulled the trigger in order to get the

Chapter Nineteen: The Try-Angle Inn Murder

cylinder to revolve; and (4) at that moment Mr. Yager, then at the desk, turned around and upon seeing the raised pistol struck defendant's arm thereby causing the weapon to discharge. Defendant said he fled only because of a panic impulse and denied aiming the gun at restaurant patrons.

Yeah! Right! As they say down south, "That dog won't hunt." Here is part of the court's ruling on his appeal;

Actually, this is one of those tragic cases where little or nothing can be said in mitigation of the irrational and violent crime here involved. The sentence imposed must stand.

The court got that right!

On September 2, 1974, the body of Adel and Dallas Center resident, Timothy Hawbaker, 18, was found in a field outside of Des Moines. He had been bludgeoned with a tire iron. Hawbaker had been in the Try-Angle Inn shortly before the murder of Richard Yager and had given testimony. It was speculated that that was somehow connected to his killing. Hawbaker's murder was later solved and no connection was found.

Lucy sold the business shortly after the tragic incident. She died in 1979 and is buried beside her husband in Oakdale Cemetery in Adel. The station soon closed but the restaurant was operated for several years after. The Try-Angle Inn is now gone. The buildings have all been demolished and nothing remains of it today.

The murder of Richard Yager was a senseless crime. What caused Smith to pull the trigger that July afternoon? Was it a robbery gone bad? Was it just that Smith and Kimmel were intoxicated and lost all sense? Was there some other reason that is not known by those who investigated this crime? Whatever the reason, a good man, a hard-working, honest, decent, friendly, well-liked man, was dead before his time. Two more lives will waste away in prison. For what??

Chapter Twenty

The Shy, Quiet Victim: Emma Lewis

It was Monday evening, September 14, 1976. Emma Lewis' friend, Phyllis Hinkson, looked at her clock and noted it was about 8 p.m., time to call Emma and remind her of a doctor's appointment the next day. The phone rang but there was no answer. Concerned but not too alarmed, Phyllis called again at 9. When there was still no answer, Phyllis drove to Emma's house. She found the porch light on and the front door open. Inside, 80-year-old Emma lay face-up on the floor near the bathroom. She had been beaten with someone's fists or a blunt object. Blood flowing from head and face wounds had blocked her nasal passages and windpipe, causing her to drown in her own blood. She had multiple face and head wounds.

Someone had apparently entered her small well-kept white frame house and beat her to death for what little money she might have had in her purse. Waukee Police, Dallas County sheriff's Officers and Iowa Bureau of Criminal Investigation (BCI) agents were baffled by the slaying. The law enforcement officials didn't find anything in the house out of place. No weapon was found. There were no signs of forcible entry and they had no suspects. They didn't even find any suspicious fingerprints. All they had were some palm prints that couldn't be used for identification. The only indication of a motive was Emma's missing purse. Investigators could not immediately determine whether Emma was beaten with fists or bludgeoned to death.

Chapter Twenty: The Shy, Quiet Victim: Emma Lewis

It was a brutal and senseless crime that had the community of Waukee upset and scared for many weeks afterward. Emma Lewis could only be described as "a sweet little lady." Standing about five foot three and weighing no more than 100 pounds, she was a shy but friendly woman. Her eyesight was failing to the point that she was almost legally blind. The widow of a coal miner, Emma was a woman of modest means. She always kept the doors locked. Clifford Applegate, a neighbor, said "I don't think I was in her house but once or twice in the 15 years we've lived next door."

There were a number of coal miner's widows living alone in Waukee and many of them were especially upset and nervous about what happened. A few were even afraid to stay alone at night.

Brick Volker, a neighbor from across the street, commented, "I can't figure out why they'd beat her that way. She was just a little bitty gal." Elaine Applegate, another neighbor, noted "She always said she hoped to stay in her home until she couldn't see to take care of herself and then she supposed she would have to go to a nursing home."

One widow in the neighborhood, Helen Leimer, 70, stayed in her son's nearby home at night and said she would until the killer was found. Mrs. Leimer, one of Emma's close friends, described Emma as a timid woman. "I go to the Senior Citizen Center, but I never could get Emma to go. It made her nervous, the crowds. She wasn't one to go out. She was a very quiet woman I don't think she ever did anybody any harm. But she was very independent too. She didn't want anything from anybody for free. I remember one time a young person took us into Des Moines for shopping and Mrs. Lewis gave me a dollar for the ride. I said, 'you give it to him,' and she said, 'well you know him better. You give it to him.' I always told the young people to take the money she offered because it made her feel better."

Emma was born September 2nd, 1896 in Hiteman, Iowa, a small coal mining town near Albia in Monroe County. Her father was killed in an accident in the Hiteman mine when she was six years old. Emma married Ivan Lewis, a coalminer, in Centerville in 1921. They lived in various Monroe County coal mining towns before moving to Waukee in the mid-1940s. Ivan passed away in 1963. They had no children. Her two surviving sisters, Sigurd Johnson, 82, of Albia and Vera Fisher, 70, of Newton- remember Emma as a very shy person who never attended social affairs and never would have hurt anyone.

Emma Lewis

Chapter Twenty: The Shy, Quiet Victim: Emma Lewis

"She was just one sweet little lady," said Mrs. Applegate. "I don't know how else you could describe her."

The case of Emma Lewis is one of the unsolved murders listed on Iowa's Cold Case website. Here are the particulars: Emma Sophia Lewis, Homicide, 80 YOA, Waukee, Iowa, Dallas County, DCI Case #76-00804, September 13, 1976. Perhaps the perpetrator of this terrible crime is still alive and could be brought to justice someday. After so many years, however, it is unlikely. That's a shame.

Chapter Twenty-One

The Murder House

A weathered two-story white farmhouse once stood along Highway 6, three miles east of Adel. It was about a quarter mile south of the highway, down an unusually long lane. It looked like so many other aging and run-down farmhouses in this part of the state, no longer the centerpiece of a farming operation but now occupied by people that earned their living off the farm. Several large mature trees provided shade in the summer and a windbreak in the winter. A large red barn, that once sheltered farm animals and stored crops, sat unused about 200 feet from the house. Between the barn and the house sat a slat-walled corncrib, the kind used before crop dryers and combines, the kind of crib that farm-boys drug corn out of and shoveled into noisy, dusty corn shellers in the middle of a cold Iowa winter. A steel windmill stood as a reminder that this homestead was here before electricity replaced wind-power on the farm. The long narrow rutted lane to the old house was bordered on each side by soybeans or corn in alternating years.

In the early 90's, the house was occupied by Jeffrey Thomas, 33, and Shari Exline, 29. They had lived in the house for about two years, along with their four-year-old son, Allen Thomas. Exline and Thomas were not married but had lived together for some time before moving into the house. Each was a known drug user and dealer in marijuana and methamphetamines.

Chapter Twenty-One: The Murder House

Thomas had worked for a time at Allstate Gutter in Waukee. He also did some odd jobs around the neighborhood. Neighbors of Thomas said he seemed like a decent guy and nobody complained about him.

Shari Exline worked in the housekeeping department at Adel Acres, a local nursing home. She had few hobbies because she worked most of the time and was devoted to her son. "She wouldn't hardly let anybody babysit him, she liked to be with him so much," her uncle, David Profitt of Centerville, said.

Melissa Maharas of Fort Dodge had been friends with Shari Exline for several years. They first met when Exline babysat for Mahara's children, Nick and Nicole, when they were young. She had started babysitting for Maharis when she was 12. Both women grew up in Fort Dodge. Nick Maharas Sr., Melissa's husband, said he and his wife remained friends with Exline over the years. "She helped Shari deal with a lot of things," he said of his wife.

Maharas had met his wife through a cousin and they had been married nearly 19 years. "There's nobody that didn't like my wife," he said. "The only people that didn't like her were people that didn't know her. Children who frequented the Hardee's restaurant where she worked knew her by name and an older customer had even sent her Flowers on her birthday."

Maharas was visiting Shari Exline in mid-July of 1991 while on vacation. Melissa Maharis was also a known drug dealer and user.

Early on the morning of Friday, July 12, 1991, neighbors noticed that every light was on in the home. Bruce Orr of Linden, a friend of Jeffery Thomas, went to the home about 6:30 a.m. to check on things. A gruesome scene greeted him when he entered the old house. Lying face down in the living room was the body of Shari Exline. It didn't take much of an examination to determine she was dead. Orr didn't stick around long after that. He jumped in his pickup and drove to the Dallas County Sheriff's Office in Adel to notify the authorities.

Murder and Mayhem in Dallas County

The Farmhouse

When officers arrived at the Thomas home, they were in for an even more gruesome sight. At the bottom of the steps leading to the basement of the home, they discovered the naked bodies of Melissa Maharis and Jeffery Thomas. Exline, Maharis, and Thomas had each been shot in the back of the head by a .25 caliber gun at close range. Maharis was dead. Thomas was badly wounded but alive. He was taken by helicopter to Iowa Methodist Medical Center in Des Moines, in critical condition.

Also in the basement, unharmed, was Allen Thomas, the four-year-old son of Thomas and Exline. The traumatized child was first taken to a foster home. He later was taken into the protective custody of state officials.

When asked if he believed an intruder was responsible, or if the case might be a murder suicide attempt, Dallas County Sheriff Jerry Tiedeman said, "We haven't ruled anything out." Sheriff's officials and

Chapter Twenty-One: The Murder House

Iowa Division of Criminal Investigation specialist spent the day pouring over the house and its surroundings. One official described the crime scene as "a mess" but declined to be more specific. Tiedeman released few details about the course of the investigation through the long day.

The bodies of the two women were removed from the house Friday afternoon and were sent to Sioux City for autopsy by state medical examiner Thomas Bennett. According to Bennett, Exline and Maharis died either late Thursday evening, July 11, 1991, or in the early morning hours of July 12, 1991. Maharis had talked to her husband by telephone about 11:37 p.m. on July 11, 1991.

Allen Thomas did not attend his mother's funeral in Centerville because he was in protective custody. Among the carnations on Exline's casket was a single pink rose that said "Mommy."

After the killings, the authorities first concentrated on David Vestal, Exline's cousin, who had formerly been in the drug business with Exline and Thomas. He had not seen them for some time but did visit the home on July 8, 1991. He told relatives later that he and Thomas had "gotten into it" during the visit. They had disagreed over drugs and money. Vestal had a history of physical violence with relatives. His girlfriend and Exline were both afraid of him.

One report, soon after the murders, said that the Dallas County Sheriff's Office would probably make an arrest that next Tuesday afternoon. That arrest never came. John Tinker, Assistant Director of the Iowa Division of Criminal Investigation, said that he was not aware of any imminent arrest. "We're not a whole lot closer than we have been. The DCI is investigating the broad possibilities of revenge, drugs or somebody's mad at somebody."

A week after the murders, the sole survivor, Jeffery Thomas, began to speak. Authorities were unable to get information from Thomas shortly after the shooting because of the severity of his wound, but now he was speaking words. Thomas was in serious condition in Iowa Methodist Medical Center where he was being guarded by Dallas County deputies.

"We're talking to him daily and he continues to improve," Tinker said. He went on to report "Thomas is lucky. The killer probably thought everyone in the house was dead. All 3 suffered a single gunshot to the head and were found bound in some way. Thomas and Maharas were found downstairs and Exline was found upstairs. One woman was found naked. Authorities won't release that name because it would be needlessly hard on a grieving family and because it could hurt the investigation. If we released too much information, we may find people making false confessions. There were no signs the women or Thomas were beaten or sexually abused."

When asked about the four-year-old boy, Tinker would only say, "It is not known if Thomas is the boy's father. Verifying who the boy's father is doesn't bear directly on the homicide investigation. That would probably be investigated later if a question of child custody arises."

"As of Wednesday, investigators had not found the weapon," Tinker added.

By mid-August, after extensive investigation, law enforcement officials had three suspects. Authorities were seeking Joey Dean Wheels, 25, whose last known address was 1225 19th St in Des Moines. Wheels was accused of first-degree murder and it appeared he had fled the area. Authorities had already arrested Troy Mure, 25, and Harris Kole Evans, 21, charging both men with two counts of first-degree murder and one count of attempted murder. All three murder suspects were thought to be connected with Des Moines area gangs. Des Moines police said Evans admitted being associated with the Vice Lords gang the previous summer. Mure and Wheels, police think, were associated with the Crips in the past and may currently be Crips members. Investigators speculated Exline, Maharas and Thomas might have been targeted for a robbery and that drugs were involved.

In early September, Joey Wheels was found in California and arrested by Los Angeles police on murder warrants issued against him by Iowa authorities. Los Angeles officials identified him as "Byron" Joey Wheels, although Iowa officials have identified him as Joey Dean

Chapter Twenty-One: The Murder House

Wheels. Dallas County Sheriff Jerry Tiedeman, a sheriff's department detective and a Division of Criminal Investigation agent flew to California to question Wheels and return him to Iowa. The group returned to Iowa Sunday evening. Wheels was arraigned the following Monday morning and pleaded innocent to the charges.

Wheels had first fled to Omaha and stayed about a week. He then returned to Des Moines for a short time before he left for California. While back in Des Moines, he had met with Mure and telephoned Evans.

The triggerman, however, was not believed to be Wheels. Troy Lee Mure was identified as shooting all three victims. The documents, prepared by Division of Criminal Investigation agents John F Quinn and Joe Diaz, indicate Mure was identified as a participant in the murders by both witness testimony and physical evidence, including fingerprints.

Other documents indicate that another defendant, Harris Cole Evans, 21, made statements to have aided and abetted in the deaths as well as critically wounding Jeffrey Alan Thomas, 33. All the victims were tied up, then shot in the back of the head, execution-style, with a .25-caliber semi-automatic pistol.

In addition to Mure and Evans, Wheels and a fourth suspect, Douglas Eugene Jones Senior, 24, were also charged with two counts of first-degree murder and one count of attempted murder. They were all held in the Dallas County jail under bonds of $550,000 each. Court documents showed it was unlikely any of the men, all listing Des Moines inner city addresses, would be able to post the bonds. All four men showed no employment, income, assets or bank accounts for the past year. They all requested that lawyers be provided for them at public expense.

Investigators still declined to release a motive for the slayings or to indicate if the shootings were the result of random violence or if the victims were specific targets. Dallas County authorities and state agents also wouldn't comment on the relationship between the victims and the men charged in the shootings.

Jeffery Thomas, who was partially paralyzed from the gunshot wound to his head, was interviewed in the presence of Jones, Evans and Mure. He gave testimony in depositions under the watchful eye of Dallas County Sheriff's Deputies and while Thomas was recovering in the hospital.

It was determined that each of the defendants would be tried separately. Wheels did some plea-bargaining. In exchange for his testimony against the other three, he would be charged with a lesser crime.

Defense lawyers for Mure contended that Jeffery Thomas was incompetent to testify. A motion filed in Dallas County District Court stated that Thomas lacked the ability to remember any relevant information and was being called as a witness only to elicit sympathy from the jury. The motion asked District Judge Peter Keller to prohibit prosecutors from calling Thomas as a witness. It stated that Thomas neither can communicate effectively nor distinguish between those things which he remembers, and those things others have told him. Keller said he would examine Thomas outside the presence of the jury to determine whether Thomas is competent.

Pre-trial motions were also made to suppress statements by Evans and Mure. Evans' lawyer claimed his client was questioned against his wishes. During questioning, Evans told a state investigator he was present when three people were shot in a farmhouse near Adel. He denied he was the triggerman but identified three others as his accomplices.

Mure's lawyer also filed a motion to suppress statements Mure made to state agents because she said his Miranda rights were violated. She also said Evans statements led police to Mure. Dallas County District Judge Peter Keller overruled the motions in a ruling in Dallas County District Court.

Maggie Moss, attorney for Mure, demonstrated why people dislike lawyers so much. She had asked District Judge Peter Keller to rule on a change of venue request, contending her client could not get a fair trial in Dallas County because of an aura of hostility and prejudice

Chapter Twenty-One: The Murder House

in the area stemming from publicity of the case. The judge was reluctant to accept her request, however. So, to prove her point she sent an investigator to the nearest tavern, which was across the street from the courthouse. He asked the afternoon patrons (not a fair sampling of the people of Dallas County by any means) what they thought of the defendants in the highly publicized case. With a few bottles of liquid courage in them and their standing in the bar's fraternity of "manly men" at stake, the patrons were more than eager to make their opinions known.

"Informal interviews with residents revealed that some were eager to take the defendants and shoot them and hang them," Moss' statement contended. "They are angry to the point of making vigilante statements."

It probably wasn't too difficult for her to get "vigilante statements" in such an environment and with such a charged question. Change of venue was granted and Mure's trial was moved to Nevada, Iowa.

Murder and Mayhem in Dallas County

Joey Wheels

Douglas Jones

Chapter Twenty-One: The Murder House

Harris Evans

Murder and Mayhem in Dallas County

Troy Mure

Chapter Twenty-One: The Murder House

After it was proven by a lawyer that Dallas County was rife with vigilantes and lynchers, trials for all defendants were moved to other counties.

Trial for Douglas E. Jones Sr., the first to be tried, commenced on January 6, 1992 in Marion County District Court in Knoxville, Iowa. His attorneys first tried to claim that it was David Vestal, and not Evans, that was the fourth man involved in the case. Allen Thomas, the four-year-old child, had identified Vestal as the "man who shot my daddy." He also picked him out of three photo line-ups. On three other photo line-ups, when Vestal's picture was not present, Allen asked, "Where was the picture of the bad man?" However, on two other occasions, Allen appeared not to recognize Vestal. Allen also said the bad man had white skin. While Thomas was in a semiconscious state in the hospital, he supposedly squeezed the hand of a law enforcement officer when asked if Vestal shot him. This was a method of identification developed by the officers.

David Vestal took the witness stand and maintained his innocence. Vestal had become the focal point of the defense strategy by lawyers on behalf of Jones. Vestal, who said he worked in the construction business, vehemently denied any involvement in the shootings. Vestal said he was at home watching television the night of the shootings. He said Robi Wilson, came to their home about 9 p.m. and they went to bed about 11. Wilson vouched for Vestal.

Vestal said he was stunned the next day to learn of the shootings while watching television. He said he went to a convenience store and called authorities to make sure the victim was his cousin. Vestal admitted dealing drugs with Exline in the past but denied ever threatening to kill her. Vestal was never arrested in connection with these crimes.

Exline's sister, Shelly Ashby, testified that about two years ago Vestal had threatened to shoot Exline during an argument. Kimberly Vestal, Vestal's sister-in-law, also had testified that Vestal telephoned her the day after the shootings and told her he recently had argued with Exline and Thomas.

Vestal said there had been no argument. He said he had visited with Exline the Monday before the shootings, and the two played pool at her house while their children played with one another.

Dallas County District Judge Peter Keller disallowed the testimony of the child psychologist of Allen Thomas. The prosecution tried to introduce the testimony to rebut earlier testimony about the child identifying Vestal from a police photo lineup. The psychologist, Barbara Cavallin of Des Moines, testified outside the presence of the jury that in August the boy pointed to a black doll when she asked him the color of his parent's attackers. Vestal is white. The four people charged in connection with the shootings are black. Keller disallowed Cavallin's testimony saying it was hearsay. Cavallin also said the child would have been dealt a set-back if he had testified during the trial.

Joey Wheels, who had agreed to testify against the others, nonchalantly told the jury he heard the gunshots that killed the two women and he had caught a glimpse of a shooting that left a man severely wounded. Wheels also testified that Jones was present when the execution style shootings occurred. Wheels, who showed little emotion while testifying, said the shootings occurred during the course of a botched drug robbery. He went on to say that he and three other men, Harris Evans, Troy Mure and Jones, participated in the robbery. In exchange for his testimony against the three other men, the prosecution allowed wheels to plead guilty to reduced charges. Wheels said he expected the deal would allow him to serve only seven years in prison instead of life.

Artis Reis, one of Jones's lawyers, attacked the credibility of Wheels during her opening statements. "He is a drug dealer who is lying to avoid a life sentence," she claimed.

Mark Smith, the other defense lawyer, repeatedly asked Wheels how he knew Jones. When Wheels said they had worked together years ago at Bakers Square Restaurant and Pie Shop, Smith brought out an earlier deposition in which Wheels had said he had not been working at that time.

Chapter Twenty-One: The Murder House

Wheels said he was delivering crack cocaine to a house on East 17th St. in Des Moines about 11 p.m. July 11th when he was flagged down by Evans and Jones. He said Evans told him of the planned drug robbery. The three men then recruited Mure to help, Wheels said. He said that on the way to the farmhouse, Jones told him if they ran into any trouble getting the drugs, they should threaten the child of Exline and Thomas. He said three guns were passed out from under a seat in the car. He took a .25 caliber pistol, Mure took a .45 caliber automatic and Jones took a .38 caliber revolver.

Wheels went on to testify that after the men entered the house, they were unable to find cocaine. They did steal some money and marijuana. Exline, Maharas and Thomas were herded down to the basement, along with the four-year-old boy. Wheels said he brought Exline back up to the living room and tied her hands behind her back with a plastic cord he had found. Evans and Mure followed him into the living room, while Jones stayed below guarding Maharas and Thomas. Exline told the men there was no cocaine and that she only sold speed.

Wheels claimed he gave his .25 caliber pistol to Evans and went upstairs to ransack the rooms up there. He said he heard a gunshot when he was leaving an upstairs bedroom. "It was definitely the .25," Wheels said. "I've shot almost every gun that there is. A .45 would have been a lot louder than that. When I reached the bottom of the stairs, I saw Exline stretched out, blood seeping from her head. Evans was walking away, the gun in his hand. Evans went into the basement. He entered into the staircase and I heard a shot. I followed Evans. He was just pointing the gun up at Jeffrey Thomas's head. I pulled my head away and heard a shot, and when I looked back Jeffrey Thomas had been shot."

After the shootings, the men returned to Des Moines and threw the gun into the Des Moines River. Wheels added that on the way back to Des Moines, Jones admitted he had forced Maharis to perform a sex act on Thomas while he was in the basement.

"I was basically paranoid," Wheels said when explaining why he later fled to California. "Because it wasn't talked about on the way out there or even thought about or mentioned that anyone was going to be murdered or anything like that. We were just supposed to take the drugs, tie them up and leave."

The defense took up much of the time in court trying to weaken the credibility of witnesses who have said they saw Jones with the other defendants near the time of the shootings. Claudia Mure, the wife of Troy Mure, testified that she saw Jones and the other defendants pick up her husband from her mother's house the night before the bodies were discovered. Michelle Curry, an acquaintance of Mure's, testified that after the shootings she saw Claudia Mure fight with Nashina A. Morrison, a cousin of Jones'. Curry said that during the fight, Claudia Mure said she would say whatever her husband told her to say. The defense contended during opening statements that Troy Mure held a grudge against Jones because Jones fathered a child with Mure's former girlfriend. During her testimony, Claudia Mure denied that she was lying about Jones.

Jurors said the most damning testimony came from Joey Wheels, who had pleaded guilty to second-degree murder. Jones' lawyer contended throughout the trial that their client was not present when the shootings occurred. Dallas County attorney David Welu told jurors in the trial, "These crimes violated everything sacred to us. This defendant and others entered our homes. They entered our private lives and violated even our sex lives."

On January 16, the Marion County jury handed down a verdict of guilty. Jones was found guilty on two counts of first-degree murder and one count of attempted murder. The first of the four to be tried, Douglas E Jones, was sentenced to two terms of life in prison with no chance of parole and was also was sentenced to 25 years for attempted murder.

Harris Evan's trial took place in Union County District Court in Creston and started on Tuesday February 11, 1992. David Welu, Dallas County Attorney, said that Evans was the triggerman and planned the

Chapter Twenty-One: The Murder House

robbery. "The evidence will show this defendant, in execution style, executed Shari Exline and Melissa Maharas and failed in an attempt on Jeff Thomas,"

Evans' lawyer, John Wellman, said Wheels, Mure and Jones were members of a street gang known as the Crips. Wellman said Evans was not a gang member. "This has been a conspiracy of the Crips against Harris Evans," Wellman said. "The men drove to the farmhouse because they believed cocaine was in the refrigerator there."

Four witnesses testified for the prosecution including Bruce Orr of Linden. Orr said he was friends with Thomas and Exline. He testified that he discovered the bodies early on the morning of July 12th.

Wheels told the jury a story that began in Des Moines and ended tragically in a farmhouse at the end of a dirt lane near Adel. Wheels said he, Evans, and two other Des Moines men participated in a plan last July to steal two kilograms of cocaine from the couple who lived at the farmhouse. He said the situation quickly escalated into violence when the cocaine could not be found. Wheels said Evans shot all three with a 25-caliber pistol.

He further stated that on July 11, 1991, he met Evans and defendant Jones in Harris's car and Harris was driving. They persuaded Wheels to join them in a plan to steal cocaine from a Dallas County farmhouse. They knew a man, woman, and child lived there. Supposedly cocaine was being kept there. They decided they needed a fourth person to assist them. They asked Ronny Walker, but he declined. Then they went in search of Troy Mure's brother. He wasn't available, and ultimately Troy agreed to help them.

To corroborate Wheels's testimony, the state produced Ronny Walker, who testified to his contact with the men. He identified photos of Harris's car used that evening. He could not recall the exact date, but said it was before he heard of the deaths in Dallas County. Mure's mother, his wife, and his uncle were present at Mure's home when defendant and the others came looking for Mure. They all identified defendant as being one of the men. Two identified a photo of Harris's car. All agreed it was during the late evening hours of July 11, 1991.

Mure's wife stated Mure left with the men about 10:30 p.m. and returned home several hours later.

Wellman attacked the credibility of Wheels, who has said he believes his plea agreement will allow him to serve only seven years in prison. Wellman said authorities furnished Wheels with the results of their entire investigation before listening to his account of what happened the night of the slayings. "They gave him an opportunity to see what they had and allowed him to adapt his statements accordingly. The state neglected to subject Wheels to a polygraph examination, which is commonly used during investigations. The state entered into an agreement with a liar and that's disturbing."

Wellman pursued a different defense than the one used by the lawyers for Jones. He acknowledged his client was present but said he tried to leave before the shootings occurred. He argued that another co-defendant, Troy Mure, forced Evans back to the house at gunpoint. Wellman argued that Mure was the triggerman.

The verdict and sentence for Evans was the same as Jones had received. Evans was convicted of two counts of first-degree murder and one count of attempted murder. Dallas County District Judge Peter Keller sentenced Evans to two terms of life in prison. Keller also sentenced Evans to 25 years in prison for attempted murder.

Wellman said he would appeal the conviction on the ground that Dallas County District Judge Peter Keller should have suppressed statements Evans made to law enforcement authorities.

Mure's trial was scheduled to begin in February but, once again, Mure's lawyer, Maggie Moss, wasn't satisfied with the venue. Nevada (Iowa) was too close to Des Moines, so she filed a motion to reconsider. Moss said media attention in the Des Moines area made it difficult for her client to have a fair trial.

This time the trial was moved to Linn County and Moss didn't even have to visit a Nevada tavern to get it changed. Trial began on April 6 In Linn County District Court in Cedar Rapids. Mure testified that he had no intention of being involved in a robbery that led to the slaying of two people and the shooting of another person. Mure testified

Chapter Twenty-One: The Murder House

that he left on the trip, that ended up at the farmhouse with three other Des Moines men, with the understanding they were going out for some beer. On the way to Adel, he found out they were going there to get some cocaine, but he understood that they were to buy the drug. Only after they got there did he figure out that the others planned to steal the drugs. He said he helped in the unsuccessful search for drugs after being told to do so, but then went back to the car. "I'm not a perfect man," Mure told the jury. "I've done wrong in my life. When I did, I would stand up and admit it. I'm also man enough to stand up for myself when I'm right. I did not kill anyone. I did not assault anyone. I did not tie anyone up. I did not take off anyone's clothes. I never had possession of a gun," he testified.

Under cross examination he said he had not told investigators, after his arrest, that he understood the purpose of going to the house was to buy drugs. Mure's mother, Carolyn Mcculler, testified that three days after the incident he woke her up about 11 p.m. to tell her he had been at the farmhouse, but he didn't do anything wrong.

Wheels, appearing uncomfortable in a suit and tie, testified that Mure was aware that the four went to the rural Adel home of Exline and Thomas to rob them of cocaine. The prosecution contended that Mure was responsible for the deaths of Exline and Maharis and the critical wounding of Thomas because the shootings were committed during a robbery in which he participated.

The defense pointed out that the shots were fired execution-style with the gun against the head of the victims. They theorized that Evans had been hired to kill the Adel residents, possibly because of a disagreement with a drug dealer related to Evans.

Mure was acquitted by the jury. Dallas County attorney David Welu had considered the Mure case the strongest of the four cases in the shootings and was surprised by the verdict.

Troy Mure's wife and mother broke into shouts and tears of joy when the verdict was read. Mure and his lawyer, Maggie Moss, hugged and sobbed.

One juror said in an interview after the verdict that he did not believe the version set out by Wheels and accepted Mure's story. "The jurors appeared to draw the same conclusions. Unanswered questions about Mure's guilt kept arising."

Defense Lawyer Moss said after the verdict that her ability to attack the credibility of Wheels was aided by his testimony at the earlier trials.

County Attorney Welu said he had not considered making a plea agreement with Mure, as he had done with Wheels. "His was the most solid case and the worst record," Welu stated, citing robbery convictions on Mure's record.

Upon being released from the Linn County jail about an hour after the verdict, Mure said he had only one comment for reporters, "Clear my name like you messed it up."

The last of the four defendants, Joey Wheels, had earlier been allowed to plead guilty to attempted murder in exchange for his testimony. He was expecting a sentence of not more than seven years. His expectations were not met. On Friday April 24, 1992 Joey wheels was ordered to serve up to 50 years in prison for his involvement in the shootings, with the possibility of parole before his term ends.

Harris Kole Evans appealed his conviction for two counts of first-degree murder and one count of attempted murder. His sentences were upheld on direct appeal in 1993. He then filed a post-conviction relief that was denied. That denial was upheld on appeal in 1999. In September of 2006, he filed a second application for post-conviction relief, alleging the change in the felony murder rule announced in another case was the basis to overturn his murder convictions. In December of 2007, he filed an amended application adding an allegation of newly discovered evidence. All of this only served to line the pockets of his lawyers. Harris Evans is still a resident of Anamosa State Men's Reformatory.

True to his word, Wellman also appealed the verdict in Douglas Jones' trial. He was no more successful than Evan's lawyers. *We have considered all the issues presented by the defendant and find no basis*

Chapter Twenty-One: The Murder House

for a reversal of defendant's conviction or sentence. The judgment of the trial court is affirmed.

When it was all over, two women had lost their lives and a child would grow up without a mother and, along with his father, suffer from both emotional and physical wounds the rest of their lives. Two men will spend the rest of their lives in prison, another will spend up to 50 years in confinement. All of this for a few dollars and some drugs.

For years after this horrendous incident, the old farmhouse stood as a reminder of the evil that men are capable of. It was known locally as the "Murder House." The house has, long since, been demolished and removed, along with the windmill and other buildings. Corn and soybeans now grow on the soil where this unspeakable crime occurred.

Chapter Twenty-Two

Gregg Nimmo

It must have been a terrible thing to watch. A female driving a pickup truck repeatedly drove down into the right-side ditch, and then circled back, crossed the road and quickly drove down into the ditch on the road's opposite side. After multiple attempts to throw a man from the truck's bed, the woman allegedly finally succeeded and then willfully ran over his body in the road, at least twice.

The pickup driver angrily jumped out of the truck, and as she stormed toward the spot behind the pickup where Nimmo lay unconscious in the road, she cursed aloud, "By God, that M—— F—— better be dead!" When it was over, Gregg Andrew Nimmo, 44, of Adel, lay motionless in the road, bleeding from head wounds.

This brutal scene took place on a gravel road near Dexter, Iowa, on Sunday, Aug. 28, 2011. It was just outside Beaver Lake Campground in Dallas County.

Several individuals allegedly witnessed the incident. Tire tracks ran up and down both ditch sides as the driver attempted to throw Nimmo from the truck and then deliberately ran him over.

Chapter Twenty-Two: Gregg Nimmo

Gregg Nimmo

An unknown person from the campground phoned the sheriff's office after the woman left the scene in her pickup. No witness, at the time, told the sheriff's office what really happened. Nimmo died two days later, on Aug. 30, 2011, at Mercy Medical Center.

With little information to go on, authorities could not determine whether Nimmo had been the victim of a hit-and-run or an accident. Witnesses later reported the truck as being in the area at the time of the incident, but at that time the Dallas County Sheriff's Office couldn't confirm the truck driver's identity or whether the person intended to hurt Nimmo. Authorities, did, however, have suspects in mind

Nimmo's family, in Newton, Iowa, maintained from the beginning that Nimmo's death was no accident, but authorities didn't have enough evidence in the case to charge anyone with a crime.

In July 2014, after nearly three years with no criminal charges, Nimmo's family sought out the help of well-known forensic pathologist Dr. Cyril Wecht. Wecht had served as a consultant in numerous high-profile cases. He said that he too believed Nimmo's death was suspicious.

According to Lt. Adam Infante of the Dallas County Sheriff's Office, a new detective took over Nimmo's case in September 2014.

Infante told the Des Moines Register newspaper, "I would love to solve it. There's just not a lot of information to act upon."

Officials purportedly now have the alleged pickup driver's name as well as names of bystanders who watched the incident unfold and watched the driver intentionally throw Nimmo from the truck before running over his body.

Linda Cook, Nimmo's sister, said she believes her brother was in the bed of a truck and that the driver deliberately "fishtailed" so that Nimmo would fall out of it. She said her brother's injuries, and the tire tracks near where his body was found, support her conclusion that the fatal injury occurred before he fell from the truck. (According to statements from those at the scene, Nimmo was killed after being thrown from the truck.)

Nimmo would have had abrasions on his body if he had fallen from a moving vehicle onto the road. He had none. Nimmo's head had been severely fractured and nearly crushed, however.

"We know he didn't accidentally fall, nor was he hit by another vehicle," Cook added. And, she thinks she knows who was driving the truck.

Unable to cope with his father's death, Nimmo's 15-year-old son, Justin A. Nimmo, took his own life eight months after the tragic incident, on May 24, 2012.

Chapter Twenty-Two: Gregg Nimmo

In efforts to help the family raise the $5,000 needed to hire Wecht to look at Gregg Nimmo's case, Clem Vestal and the "515 Riders Motorcycle Club" hosted a "Justice for Gregg and Son" potluck dinner and silent auction on Sunday, Oct. 19, 2014 at the "Maingate Bar and Grill" in Des Moines.

"My main goal is just to help lift the spirits. Just show them, Man, there's people out there that don't even know you, but we care," Vestal said.

The Nimmo family has set up a fund at US Bank, also called "Justice for Gregg and Son," and donations may be made at any branch.

Gregg Nimmo was an organ donor, and his family has the comfort of knowing he lives on in the life-saving gifts he gave to others.

This is a case that could easily be solved. It just takes that one clue or bit of information. Somewhere out there there's a woman who drives a pickup (or did in 2011), has a terrible temper and knows some pretty foul langauge.

Anyone with information about Gregg Nimmo's unsolved death is urged to contact the Iowa Division of Criminal Investigation at (515) 725-6010, or call the Dallas County Sheriff's Office at (515) 993-4771 or email dcsheriff@co.dallas.ia.us.

Murder and Mayhem in Dallas County

Chapter Twenty-Three

Sheriffs of Dallas County

Chapter Twenty-Three: Sheriffs of Dallas County

First Sheriff Eli Smithson
1847 J.K. Miller
1847 E. Smithson
1849 S. Marrs
1850 H. Morrison
1850 W. Ellis
1850 I.C. Hughes
1852-1855 Not Listed
1855 S.C. Taylor
1857 I.D. Marsh
1862 W. Ellis
1862 J.M. Byers
1871 A.W. Haines
1875 S.J. Ellis
1877 J.W. Bly
1881 S. Adams
1884 J.W. Diddy
1890 S.S. Zenoa
1894 J.D. Payne
1900 Joe Hanes
1907 George Ross
1912 G.H. Ross
1916 Chas V. McGriff
1920 J.W. Stacy
1924 S.J. Nuzum
1928 S.J. Nuzum
1932 C.A. Knee
1936 C.A. Knee
1940 No results available

1944 Evan A. Burger
1948 Evan A. Burger
1952 Evan A. Burger
1956 Evan A. Burger
1960 Evan A. Burger
1964 John T. Wright
1968 John T. Wright
1972 John T. Wright
1976 Robert DeCamp
1980 Lee Struble
1984 Lee Struble
1988 Jerry Tiedeman
1992 Arthur L. Johnson
1996 Arthur L. Johnson
2000 Arthur L. Johnson
2004 Brian Gilbert
2006 Kevin Frederick
2007 (Special Election)   Chad W. Leonard
2008-Present   Chad W. Leonard

Chapter Twenty-Three: Sheriffs of Dallas County

Current Dallas County Sheriff Chad Leonard

Murder and Mayhem in Dallas County

The first official office to be filled in Dallas County was that of sheriff. In order to organize Dallas County, it was first necessary for the state legislature to appoint a sheriff who would serve until the first elections could be held. Sheriff Eli Smithson was duly appointed, and a special election was provided for to be held on the first Monday of April 1847. At this first election, it was necessary to elect three county commissioners, one county commissioners' clerk, one clerk of district court, one treasurer and recorder, a sheriff, a surveyor, a judge of probate, a prosecuting attorney, a coroner, a sealer of weights and measures, and a school fund commissioner, with the required number of justices of the peace and constables.

There were two polling places named in the sheriff's proclamation, one at the house of W. W. Miller, located at the edge of the prairie on the north side of the road leading east, and about two miles distant from Adel. The other was at the house of Henry Stump in Boone Township.

Jesse K. Miller was duly elected sheriff at this first political event, without putting up a single yard sign. The first election for sheriff was a spirited one, spirited in a double sense, as the successful candidate, Jesse Miller, not only made an ardent campaign to get votes to espouse his cause, but also strengthened his chances by liberal donations of ardent spirits.

Our first sheriff, Eli Smithson, died 30 Aug 1851 at the ripe old age of 36 years 4 months and 29 days. He is buried in the Miller Cemetery. His son Newton was the first white child born in Dallas county.

The new county had difficulty keeping their elected sheriffs from running off to the gold fields in California during those first years. Samuel Marrs had just been elected in 1849 when he got the gold fever and sold his 160-acre claim in Washington Township to D.M. Starbuck for $150. By 1850, the county had grown enough to have three voting precincts, Penoach, Boone and Des Moines. There were, in all, 92 votes cast for the next sheriff, of which Horatio Morrison (Whig) received 55, Thomas Butler (Dem.) received 36, and Eli Smithson received 1

Chapter Twenty-Three: Sheriffs of Dallas County

vote, giving Morrison a majority of 19 votes, and therefore duly electing him sheriff. Here's how Morrison was described by an early news account:

The sheriff elect came here from Missouri with a large family in 1848 and is described by one who knew him well as being "a genial, wholesouled, kindly, loquacious, vis a vis sort of a man, who to be known was to be respected. But alas for poor humanity! The "social glass," one of the engines of satan to polute and destroy God's noblest work and world, beset his pathway and quickened his footsteps to the threshold of eternity. Morrison held the office only a few months, he too having resigned, and, in company with his son James, went to California in the spring of 1850, a 'gold-hunter, where he died a few years later."

W. Ellis was the next to be elected to fill the remainder of the term and he did just that. At the next regular election, 1850, Irwin C. Hughes was elected sheriff of Dallas County.

One of the more amusing incidents regarding our previous sheriffs happened to Steven Adams, who served from 1881 to 1884. Here's the story as reported:

Steve was a good honest citizen, somewhat unsophisticated and careless of dress, but withal a very worthy man. It seems that his first important official duty after being inducted into office was to convey to the penitentiary a smooth, polished criminal named Bumpus, who had been convicted for defrauding the farmers by selling them a bug powder, getting their notes under false representations and selling t-hem to innocent purchasers. As Bumpus was a very docile prisoner, Sheriff Adams did not handcuff him, and when they arrived at Fort Madison, Bumpus attempted to turn the sheriff over to the penitentiary authorities, and as he was a pretty smooth fellow and gifted with a persuasive tongue, he came pretty near succeeding. The fact that Mr. Adams had the handcuffs in his pocket was a presumption in 'favor of the truth of his claims and after some other corroborating facts and considerable parley, the real criminal was incarcerated, and Adams allowed to return. This story has been told and retold many times at Mr. Adams' expense, and while it seemed rather laughable to him in after years, it came very near being anything but a joke to him at the time.

Sheriff J.D. Payne, who served from 1894 to 1900, acted honorably and heroically after the robbery of the Adel State Bank in 1895. His brave efforts prevented the lynching of a young man who had made a mistake but went on to live a useful and productive life.

Sheriff Charles V. McGriff kept order in the county through the difficult days of WW1 and the Spanish Flu Epidemic.

Sheriffs J.W. Stacy and Samuel J. Nuzum had the thankless task of enforcing the unpopular and often ignored prohibition laws.

Dallas County Sheriff Clint Knee was so well known after capturing Clyde Barrow in the Bonnie and Clyde raid at Dexfield Park that he was offered the position of the first chief of the Iowa State Patrol when that body was established in 1933.

Sheriff Evan A. Burger was Dallas County's longest serving sheriff. He was first elected in 1944 and served four terms ending in 1960.

There are many more stories of the brave men who served as Dallas County Sheriffs and Deputies in the past almost 175 years. Most of these men have proved to be dedicated and capable officials who have played a large role in making Dallas County one of the best places to live on this planet.

End

Made in the USA
Monee, IL
07 January 2021